The Early Years
Gardening Handbook

by Sue Ward

Illustrations by Cathy Hughes
Published by Practical Pre-School Books
St Jude's Church, Dulwich Road, Herne Hill, London, SE24 0PB
Tel. 020 7738 5454
www.practicalpreschoolbooks.com
© MA Education 2010

The Early Years Gardening Handbook ISBN: 978 1 907241 04 8

Why should young children be involved in gardening?

The Early Years Foundation Stage (2007) refers to the positive impact of time spent outdoors for children's development and sense of wellbeing. Outdoor environments offer children freedom to explore, use their senses, and be physically active. Young children are active learners with a natural curiosity that requires them to have hands-on contact with the real world. Involvement in gardening gives them purposeful opportunities to explore, investigate and discover new things.

Access to a garden and opportunities to contribute to what is grown there, can boost children's self-esteem and encourage them to develop a greater understanding of the role they play in caring for the world around them. They learn to take responsibility for living things and will hopefully develop a life-long respect for nature. Children who spend regular time within the garden frequently show higher levels of engagement and motivation than when indoors.

Through gardening, there are many enjoyable ways to meet the aims of Every Child Matters (2004).

Be healthy

It is impossible to create a thriving garden without getting active and children will generally love the opportunity to get involved in activities such as digging and watering plants. Growing their own crops and cooking them will help children develop their understanding of healthy eating choices, and they will often be prepared to try new foods that they have grown.

Stay safe

Children need to understand what is acceptable when using the garden. For example, they must learn to handle tools appropriately, know when it is safe to taste plants and take steps to stay safe when outdoors in all types of weather.

Over recent years educational settings have become increasingly interested in inspiring children to become involved in gardening. The focus has often been on older, school-aged children who are more suited to approaching the garden in similar ways to adults. There has been very little support for professionals looking to involve younger children in exciting and beneficial gardening activities. An early years garden is most effective when it meets the specific needs of the under fives, both in its design and the way it is used.

Enjoy and achieve

Gardens are constantly changing with the seasons and are excellent resources for learning. They provide opportunities to develop concentration skills, problem-solving and decision-making. Children of all abilities can develop a greater understanding of the seasons, the weather and how food grows through first-hand experiences.

Make a positive contribution

Gardening helps young children understand their place within the world and the impact they have upon it. It creates opportunities for social interactions and the development of relationships between peers and across different generations. Through gardening, children will learn about developing personal qualities, such as patience and respect; they will also learn to work independently and within a team.

Achieve economic well-being

'Growing' projects can help young children understand basic concepts around the use of money. For example, they will learn that seeds are purchased and the produce from these seeds can be sold to the local community to generate more funds to support further development of the garden.

Gardening activities link well to the Early Years Foundation Stage. There is a section at the end of this book (see pages 54-62) that provides a selection of activities, all of which fulfil several of the Early Learning Goals.

Developing a garden will give the children in your care the chance to have many wonderful and memorable experiences. The impact of the outdoors is sometimes undervalued but we owe it to the next generation to give them a range of opportunities connected with the natural world.

Getting started

Home links

Involve parents and carers from the start. A regular garden newsletter will help to get the whole community more involved and should hopefully lead to offers of support and donations.

Getting a team together

Before you launch into enthusiastic digging of beds or blow your budget on packets of seeds with fantastic pictures on the front, it is wise to first stop and to consider who is going to manage the gardening project, both now and in the future. Perhaps you are a keen gardener who wants to share the pleasures of gardening with the children in your care, or maybe someone has selected you as an 'outdoors' person to get the garden underway. However you have become involved, it is important that you form a group of interested individuals to develop the project, make decisions and share the workload. This will also help to ensure that the garden continues to thrive in the future, even when there are changes in staff.

Start by talking to as many people as possible about your ideas for the garden and how it will benefit the children. Staff members in particular need an opportunity to voice their concerns early on. Perhaps they see it as extra work on top of an already busy workload, or they may be concerned that they will be expected to get cold or dirty. As the project develops, you will hopefully find some willing volunteers to get involved. Send a flyer home to parents or create a display board which can be adapted over time

as the garden grows. And of course, talk about your ideas with the children since their enthusiasm can often be a driving force.

You may wish to carry out a skills audit. This will enable you to discover different ways in which people can contribute to the development of the garden. Some of the skills which might be needed include:

- Basic DIY – laying slabs, carpentry, painting etc
- Landscape design
- Gardening – both labouring and knowledge of plants
- Fundraising
- Finding and applying for grants
- Cooking

Ask for useful contacts which can be used to help resource the garden such as a parent who works in a local garden centre or who has access to cheap building materials. If you have keen gardeners amongst your community, encourage them to grow a few extra plants at home which can then be planted in the garden once it is ready.

You can spread the work load by allocating members of the project team a range of roles. Different people will naturally be suited to taking on different responsibilities so first identify what areas of work need to be covered. The main areas might include;

Project coordinator: Although this role can seem the most daunting, this person may simply be responsible for keeping track of the overall progress of the project and arranging regular meetings. In practice, there is often a single person who will ensure that the project continues to be driven forward and who takes responsibility for ensuring that all members of the project team understand and fulfil their allocated tasks.

Fundraising coordinator: This may be an individual or a team of people who have the task of finding suitable funding to support the garden development. They will need to investigate external grants or competitions and will also be responsible for contacting local businesses and organisations to ask for donations. They may also head up the group who organise fundraising events amongst parents and the local community. You may wish to have a separate individual to take responsibility for the finances, monitoring the incomings and outgoings once the project is underway.

Communication/publicity: Communication is vital both within the setting, in keeping people informed and helping to maintain momentum, as well as within the wider community via the local press.

Fact-finder: Once again, this role is probably best taken on by a group of people who coordinate the collection of information needed in the planning and creation of a successful garden. It might include visiting other settings, attending training opportunities, ordering brochures or scouring websites for inspiration.

What have we already got?

Many settings may already have an area used for growing. This may be little more than a couple of pots or you might be fortunate enough to have ready prepared beds. Some settings will have an area so overgrown that no one has ventured into it for years whereas others may be faced with a newly created outdoor area, perhaps simply tarmac or grass. Whatever your situation it is important that you stop and ask a range of questions before planning your new garden. This will ensure that you make the best use of what you already have and it will give you valuable information for when you are drawing up your designs.

Some of the questions you might need to ask include:

How big is the area?

Many settings will have little control over the space which they can allocate to a growing area. However, if you are able to create the boundaries of your garden, first consider the number of children who might be accessing the area at any one time and think about how much space they will require.

If you are fortunate enough to have a large outdoor area, it might be tempting to create a garden the size of an allotment. However it is important that you consider whether you have the necessary time and manpower to maintain an area of that size. Also, begin to think about what you will be using your garden for. If planting

is a priority, you will need beds or planters of a sufficient size to hold all that you hope to grow. It is often best to start slowly and gradually increase your growing area as confidence increases so make sure that you have the space to do so.

What features do we already have?

If you are developing a previously used garden, you may wish to keep some existing features. These might include paths, trees, shrubs, sheds, seating or beds. However, ensure that you have thought about what did and did not work in that area as it may be more effective in the long-term to redesign the garden to best suit your needs. Sometimes features can be lifted and repositioned to better effect. It may be possible to renovate a shed and save valuable funds, replacing it at a later date.

How accessible is it?

Consider the position of your proposed garden in respect to your indoor area and any other outdoor spaces. Can you

access it all year round or will you struggle to cross muddy ground? Ensure that any fences or gates that you are planning do not restrict access to other areas.

Where is it situated?

A garden is ideally positioned where it can be easily seen so that everyone can enjoy watching how it changes from one season to the next. It is also less likely to become neglected if it is highly visible as you are more likely to notice when things need doing. Consider what impact the weather might have on what you are growing. Does most of the growing area receive sun throughout the day? Are you exposed to strong winds? Are you planning to plant in dry soil beneath trees, or does the ground become waterlogged for much of the year?

How safe is it?

Staff should be very familiar with carrying out safety assessments so apply the same approach to the area you wish to develop.

Keeping children safe in the garden is considered in a later chapter but at this stage think about the safety of those features you want to keep. Are paths slippery or uneven? Are there branches sticking out at a child's eye-level or especially prickly shrubs? Is the area fenced? Are there any existing water features?

How secure is it?

It is particularly upsetting to spend time nurturing a garden only to have someone needlessly destroy what you have carefully grown. Sadly many settings experience damage to their outside areas and will already be taking what precautions they can. To help avoid this happening, encourage the local community to take pride in the garden and report sighting of unwanted visitors. Invest in secure storage for tools and attach garden furniture to the ground where possible. Most importantly, do not give up. If plants are uprooted, replant as soon as possible - a gardener soon learns to be resilient!

Are there any services running through the site?

Ensure that you check any plans you might have for evidence of existing services such as gas or water pipes running through the site. You are unlikely to disturb them unless you are planning

foundations or very deep digging but it is safer to be aware before expensive accidents happen.

Do we have access to water?

No garden can survive without water so an easily accessed supply of water is vital. Ideally a tap situated within the garden area will simplify the watering process and avoid floors becoming soaked as watering cans are dragged from indoors. You may already have a water butt or a suitable sloping roof to collect water from.

Which way does the garden face?

Consider how the sun travels over the garden throughout the day. Beds should ideally be positioned so that the long lengths run north to south as this will maximize the sunshine which the plants receive.

What type of soil do we have?

The soil you use will influence how successfully plants grow. You may be planning to use your existing soil in which case you

can either select plants best suited to the conditions which it provides, or you can attempt to modify it.

The main variables to be aware of are pH and soil structure. Soils may be acidic (usually a pH of 5.5 - 6.5), neutral (pH 7) or alkaline (pH 7.5 - 8). You can test your soil simply using a cheap kit readily available from garden centres. Children love this as it involves mixing soil with the chemicals supplied in the kits which then change colour as if by magic. Most plants prefer a soil which is neither too acidic nor too alkaline with a pH of around 6.5. Ericaceous compost can be bought to provide more acidic soil, suitable for rhododendrons and strawberries, whereas the addition of agricultural lime will create a more alkaline soil best suited to cabbages and broccoli. However, as long as your soil is not at either extreme, the majority of what you plant should grow without too many problems. The addition of organic matter such as compost or well-rotted manure will help to dilute the effects of extreme acidity or alkalinity. It will also improve the structure of the soil, feed the plants and help to retain water. By feeling the soil you should be able to determine whether you have an especially sandy or clay soil. Since the solution to both

is the regular addition of organic matter, it is useful to create a composting area as soon as possible.

Do we have anywhere for storage?

You are going to need somewhere secure and easily accessible to store tools, seeds etc. You may wish to invest in a shed or allocate space in an existing area. Garden centres now stock a range of storage solutions in different sizes and materials.

Does the area have multiple uses?

Some settings choose to keep a garden area separate from other existing outdoor spaces and visit with groups of children to carry out specific tasks. However, your garden may form part of a larger outdoor provision, particularly if its primary purpose is to provide somewhere for children to go and have close contact with the natural world. If you wish to develop a growing area, you will need to consider how you will ensure that children do not enthusiastically dig up what you planted the day before. Careful explanation when planting can help to avoid this. Involve children in creating signs for especially vulnerable plants warning others to look carefully but not to touch. Children love to dig, so saving an area of soil specifically for digging and watering will give them an opportunity to practice their skills.

Who is currently responsible for maintenance?

Ensure that you have spoken to the person currently responsible for maintaining the garden area. They may have concerns that your development will present them with a huge amount of extra work. Reassure them that this is not the case and that you plan to involve the children as far as possible in looking after the garden on a regular basis. If any additional maintenance is required, you will need to agree what will be needed and how often.

Do we have to get permission to make changes?

Before you start, make sure that you are clear about who owns the land you are planning to develop and whether there are any restrictions as to how it can be used. Check for rights of way across the land and records of conservation or tree preservation orders which might affect what you are able to do. Consider whether there may be future plans to develop your setting as you do not want to position your garden in any area which might be the proposed site for a building extension.

How do people feel about the area?

It is important to consider how a garden development might impact on both those within and neighbouring your setting. If the project involves the renovation of a previously used garden, think about the feelings of those involved in the original project. Do they still have contact with the setting? Do they wish to be involved, on the understanding that maybe your plans might be different this time round?

You may have immediate neighbours that overlook the site. If the garden is within an existing outdoor area, its development is more likely to be welcomed than cause offence as it will probably enhance the appearance of the area. However, if you are planning to develop a previously unused area such as at the end of a field, this may create additional disturbance for those adjacent to the area. Avoid confrontation by informing neighbours early on about your plans and stress the benefits to them, such as a more attractive outlook or increased wildlife. Invite your neighbours to become involved in the project – they might be invaluable if you are closed at certain times of the year and need someone to assist with watering. If you are planning to develop an area which is presently used by the children, involve them in the process of surveying the site.

They probably know the space better than anyone and can provide invaluable information about what is there and how they feel about it. Consultation with young children is hopefully something embedded into daily practice at your setting and you may already have tried and tested ways of eliciting the views of the children in your care. Learning Through Landscapes, the national school grounds charity, has promoted the involvement of children in grounds development. For more information explore their website which is listed in the resources at the end of this book.

Consultation activities include:

- Let individuals or small groups of children walk an adult around the area and talk about what they do or do not like. They might want to record their ideas on a voice recorder or make 'notes' on a clipboard. Very young children might feel more comfortable using a soft toy or puppet as an intermediary, sharing their thoughts with them rather than an adult.

- Stickers or post-it notes can be prepared in advance with happy and sad faces. The children can then use these to attach to areas or objects which they wish to keep as part of the garden development, or would like to see removed or changed.

- Digital cameras are an excellent way for children to keep a record of their outdoor area and can be used as a valuable stimulus for discussion later on.

Planning the garden

What is the purpose of the garden?

■ Many early years practitioners rush to create a new garden area without stopping to think about how it will be used. Before starting, sit down with the project team and identify the main purpose of the garden. Consider the various ages and abilities of the children in your care. What type of home environments do they come from and to what extent are they exposed to the natural world?

■ Look at the other indoor and outdoor spaces within your setting and how they are used. For example, you may want to create a 'wild' garden where children can take risks, exploring and hiding from others. If you have experimented with growing produce in pots, now might be the time to invest in a larger growing area. Where do the children go when they want time to themselves? A garden can provide a valuable space to relax and think.

Collecting ideas

Inspiration can come from many sources. Once you have developed initial ideas about the features to include in the garden, conduct a fact-finding mission to further develop your ideas.

Home links

Share out several disposable cameras among the children. Allow each child to take a camera home for a few days. Encourage them to take photographs of features within their own home or local environment, which they would like to include in the final design of the setting's garden.

■ Visit other settings that have already developed a garden. Use their ideas as a starting point for what would or would not work in your outdoor area. The Garden Organic website (www. gardenorganic.org.uk) allows you to search for nearby settings that have already started to develop a growing area.

■ Talk to keen gardeners about what they have successfully done in their own gardens.

■ Look through gardening books and magazines for ideas to suit your own environment and budget.

■ Search the internet. There are many excellent websites that give inspiration and ideas. A list of relevant websites is provided at the back of this book.

■ Seek out parents or members of the local community, such as professional gardeners and builders, who can share their expertise.

Hard landscaping

'Hard landscaping' describes garden design made from construction materials, such as paths and raised flower beds. This is usually the most expensive part of a project and is hardest to change if you do not get it right first time.

Paths

■ Firstly consider what function the paths are going to play. For example: Do they allow people to use the garden area in all

types of weather? Do they encourage children to travel in a particular direction? This will influence the materials used and the path layout.

- The materials selected will be influenced by a range of factors including cost, durability, accessibility and appearance. Grass is attractive and cheap but is not especially hard-wearing and can often become water-logged in the winter months. Bark and gravel are cheap and easy to lay down but they will need to be topped up annually. Bark and gravel also spread easily and can become a toilet area for local cats!

- Slabs may be the most suitable choice, although they will vary in price range depending on whether you opt for concrete or natural stone. Like wood, they can also become slippery in wet weather.

- Other options, perhaps for smaller garden areas, are stepping stones, cobbles and even glass chippings or shells.

- Ensure that paths are wide enough. They should be at least 120cm to allow wheelchairs through. Check for obstructions along the path, such as outward opening windows or doors, which could prove hazardous.

- If the path consists of different height levels, consider including a series of steps or a gently sloping ramp.

Beds

- It will be necessary to include at least one growing bed in your garden design (unless you will only be planting in containers).

- Some beds can be filled with permanent planting which does not need to be replaced regularly such as a sensory area or herb garden.

- If the bed will be used to grow food crops, create narrow plots (about one metre wide) that are accessible from both sides. These are ideal for young children as they can easily reach the middle.

- Raised beds are less likely to be walked upon and are generally easier to reach. They are usually made from timber (use ready treated timber rather than old railway sleepers, which can often ooze tar in hot weather). Fill the beds with a thick layer of wet newspaper or cardboard and then build up layers using organic material, such as straw, grass clippings, garden compost, well-rotted manure and bought compost, ensuring that the top layer is made of fine compost suitable for planting.

- Position the beds so that the long lengths run north to south (to receive maximum sunlight). Plant in rows running east to west across the bed, with the tallest crops placed at the northern end so that they do not cast shadows over the other plants.

Other structures

- You may wish to introduce other permanent structures into your garden setting. For example, a wooden pergola can provide support for climbing plants and valuable shade on a hot summer's day. Alternatively, posts might be required to support temporary fabric sails, which can shade a large number of children at once.

- A permanent work area for the children can be useful when sowing seeds or potting up plants. It also creates a place for listening, somewhere to focus the children's attention without the distraction of the rest of the garden. You might want a range of informal seating where children and staff can stop and enjoy the garden. You could also look at purchasing a small potting shed or greenhouse.

Drawing up plans

Once you have gathered your ideas, it is time to draw up a more detailed plan. Some early years settings are fortunate enough to a have a garden designer but unless you wish to pay for professional advice, you will need to create a finished design.

- Most garden areas are fairly simple, and you should now be able to position the different features to create a functional and attractive layout. Try out your design by chalking it out in the proposed space, using a range of objects, such as ropes and boxes to represent the different elements. The children should be able to help with this and you will soon get a feel for how the design works in practice.

- Alternatively, you could involve the children by creating a model of the garden, allowing them to develop a greater understanding of what the finished area may look like.

An example plan is provided on page 17 to offer ideas of features you may want to consider including in your own garden.

Finding funding

It is always difficult to know which should come first – the funding or the plans. Without sufficient money, there can be little development. Exciting plans for a new garden can inspire people to find imaginative ways to generate the funds needed. Also, many grant applications will want details of what you are planning to do before you submit the application. It is generally better to seek out sources of funding at the same time as planning your garden project.

The more people who are involved in the garden project, the more successful your fundraising is likely to be. Support does not have to be financial; look to parents and local businesses for donations of goods or services. Explain what you are planning, how they could help and how it might benefit them. Find imaginative ways to generate funds, such as running your own plant sales or auctioning offers of help to mow lawns or water plants.

There are many different sources of financial funding available for garden developments and it is vital to research them thoroughly. This will enable you to select the ones most suited to your project. Allocate this role to someone from your planning team, preferably someone who feels confident in searching the internet. Here are some points to be aware of when applying for larger grants, particularly those funded by the National Lottery:

- Many grants require you to demonstrate a clearly identifiable need for the garden and to have measurable outcomes such as the number of children or families involved.

- Some grants are only available to charitable bodies. Contact The Charity Commission for England and Wales (www.charity-commission.gov.uk) for guidance on registering.

- Consider how the wider community might access the garden on an occasional basis as this is often a requirement from funding bodies.

- Establish how you will fund the ongoing maintenance of the garden.

- Be aware of the timescale of the grant. Are you able to wait for a number of months before you start work or do you require more immediate funding?

- Competitions are a fun way to secure additional funds. Remember that the widely publicised national competitions may have more entrants, meaning that there is less chance of success but it might be worth the attempt so do not be dissuaded.

Sample letter

On the following page is an example of a letter that you could send to parents and the local community to raise support and donations for your project. Adapt it to suit your setting.

The Daffodil Nursery

Dear Parents/Friends of The Daffodil Nursery,

We are very excited to be planning a new garden area for the nursery. This will provide the children with many stimulating opportunities to grow a whole range of plants, many of which they can cook and eat.

We want everyone to feel part of this venture and would like to invite you to get involved.

Here are some of the ways in which you could help:

- Do you have any special skills that you could offer, such as building, carpentry or gardening? We are looking for both expert advice and practical help.

- We will be holding a working party-day and we will need volunteers to help with digging beds and providing refreshments.

- Can you offer any donations? We will circulate a list of what we need in a few weeks but if you are a keen gardener, perhaps you have some seedlings or pots to spare. Also, we will be asking local businesses to support this project, so any valuable contacts you have would be of great help.

We are sure that the children will let you know what is happening but for more information do pop in for a chat or keep an eye on the Daffodil Garden noticeboard in the entrance.

Thank you for your support and we look forward to enjoying our new garden this summer.

The Daffodil Nursery

Example of a garden plan

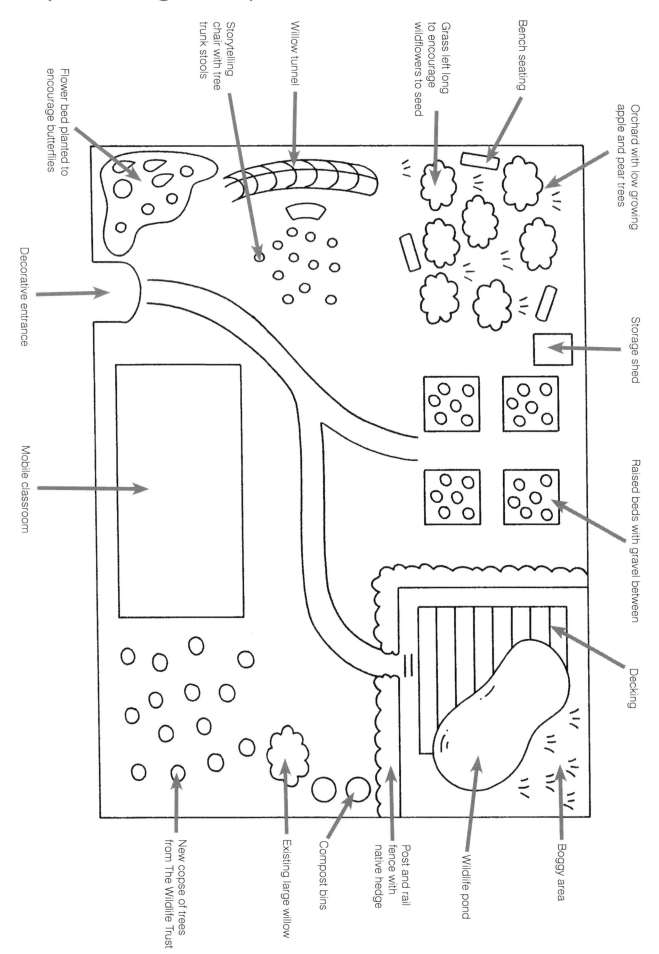

Flower bed planted to encourage butterflies

Storytelling chair with tree trunk stools

Willow tunnel

Grass left long to encourage wildflowers to seed

Bench seating

Orchard with low growing apple and pear trees

Decorative entrance

Storage shed

Mobile classroom

Raised beds with gravel between

Decking

Boggy area

New copse of trees from The Wildlife Trust

Existing large willow

Compost bins

Post and rail fence with native hedge

Wildlife pond

Planning Checklist

Use this checklist to plan and chart your progress in planning the garden. Fill it in each time you meet, initially brainstorming ideas and record what you have done as the garden plans get underway.

Date:		
Planning activities	**Comments**	**Started**
Publicise the project		
Form a project team and allocate roles		
Carry out a skills audit		
Survey the proposed area		
Collect ideas		
Identify what we want to do in the garden		
Investigate funding		
Draw up a detailed plan		
Share plans		

Month by month garden guide

January

It is likely to be cold and damp outside at this time of year, so stay in the warm and plan for the year ahead. Look at seed catalogues and nursery websites for inspiration of what grow. Don't be afraid to try something new!

Prune fruit trees and cut all raspberry canes down to ground level.

Start fundraising to support the development of your garden this year. Perhaps you could share your progress as funds are collected by creating a wall display with paper sunflowers or beanstalks which 'grow' to represent the amount of money being raised.

February

February is an ideal time to have a sort out in your shed. Wash out pots and seed trays to reduce the risks of young seedlings developing diseases and ensure that tools are clean and sharpened.

Give early varieties of seed potatoes a good start by chitting them now. Chitting is the process by which plants develop shoots indoors before they are planted out into soil. Stand them in cardboard egg boxes, ensuring that the end with the most shoots is facing upwards, and leave on a window ledge for a few weeks.

If you have an indoor growing area or greenhouse, begin to sow lettuce now for an early salad crop.

March

Don't be tempted to start growing outside too early. Consider your local conditions, such as where in the country you live, and keep an eye on the weather. If seeds are sown too early before the soil has had a chance to warm up, they are likely to just sit in the soil, or even rot.

Now is an ideal time to add additional growing areas to your garden. Start digging out new areas for planting.

If you have a warm windowsill or propagator, you can now start sowing tomato seeds. Consider choosing small varieties such as Gardeners Delight, ideal for tiny mouths!

April

Hopefully the weather is now improving and you are managing to use the outdoors more. Now you should be able to start sowing many of the early vegetables such as broad beans, radishes, carrots and salad leaves.

Strawberries can be planted out now. If you have new plants which are only a year old, remove the flowers so that no fruit is produced this year. Although this may be disappointing it will help to ensure larger crops in following years.

Slugs and snails will be starting to appear, eager to begin munching their way through your young seedlings and plant leaves. Develop a plan of action to keep their numbers down. Try a yoghurt pot pushed into the ground with the top just above the surface and a little milk at the bottom. The slugs will climb in to drink the milk but will be unable to escape again and will drown.

May

You should be very busy in the garden this month and the weeds will be growing fast. Some weeds are easily picked out by hand but others, such as dandelions, have long roots and if these snap when you are trying to remove them, they are likely to grow into a new plant.

Build wigwams from canes or willow withies for beans and sweet peas to grow up. These add height to the garden and make an attractive centrepiece to a vegetable bed.

Sow sweetcorn indoors in cardboard tubes which can then be planted out directly into the soil when the risk of frost has passed.

June

Early varieties of carrots, potatoes, lettuce and peas may now be ready for harvesting. Develop numerical skills through counting, weighing and measuring.

Plant up hanging baskets and containers with colourful bedding plants for an instant cheerful display. Add interest by including herbs such as thyme or chives, or plant some trailing tomatoes such as Tumbler. Water retaining granules can be added to the soil to help retain moisture if you are unable to water at the weekends.

July

If the weather is warm and there is little rain, ensure that you are watering regularly. Use small watering cans to give lots of children the chance to get involved without drowning delicate new plants.

Broad beans may be attracting blackfly. Remove the growing tips to help reduce this and spray pests with a diluted solution of washing up liquid. Alternatively, plant nasturtiums close as these should attract blackfly away from your beans.

If you let some of your peas and beans mature on the plants, they will eventually dry out and can be picked, stored and sown the following year.

August

Some settings may close over August, so organise a rota of people to continue to care for the garden.

Plant out cabbages and cauliflowers now and sow a hardy lettuce variety such as Valdor for winter use. If you are growing tomatoes, they will need regular feeding and watering. By removing the growing tips, you will focus the plant's energy on producing tomatoes rather than more leaves.

Remember to keep turning your compost if possible, as the warmth will help it to break down more quickly. Water occasionally if it begins to dry out.

September

The summer is now drawing to a close and if you are lucky you may have an Indian summer with clear blue skies and warm days. Now is a fantastic time to harvest fruit. You may be fortunate to have a bumper crop of apples, pears, blackberries, plums or autumn raspberries. All of which are perfect for making delicious crumbles, pies or even a summer pudding.

Early September is the time to sow green manures. These will help to preserve the fertility of the soil over the winter months and will also keeps weeds at bay, saving you time and energy in the spring. Try sowing Hungarian grazing rye which will grow slowly over the next few months and can then be dug over and allowed to rot down next March.

October

October is the month to tidy your beds. Once your crops or bedding plants have been removed, dig over the beds to loosen the soil. This will help the frost to break up the soil further making it easier to handle the following year.

Plant garlic now for a better crop. Is it not necessary to buy bulbs from a garden centre as those from the supermarket will do just as well. Break off the largest cloves and plant with the pointed end just below the surface of the soil. Space each clove about 10cm apart. Harvest the following summer when the foliage has started to turn yellowy-brown.

November

Now is an excellent time to make leaf mould using leaves from deciduous trees. This can be used to improve the texture of the soil and also makes a very good mulch when spread on top of the soil to restrict the growth of weeds. Collect fallen leaves in black plastic bags, water if they are dry and store somewhere out of sight for a couple of years until the leaves have broken down.

Rhubarb plants can be bought from the garden centre now and planted for harvesting the follow spring. The plants, known as crowns, should be positioned just under the surface of the soil and covered with a layer of organic matter. Please remember that although the stems are delicious cooked with a little brown sugar, the leaves are poisonous if eaten.

December

Many forms of wildlife, such as hedgehogs, squirrels, mice and insects will be looking for shelter from the cold. Consider creating a corner of your garden to offer them somewhere to make their winter homes. A pile of logs, sticks and leaves is ideal or think about buying a purpose-made animal home.

A large number of vegetables are now ready for harvesting, in preparation for a Christmas feast. Now is the time to harvest brussels sprouts, leeks, parsnips and cauliflowers.

Now is also an ideal time to plant bare-rooted fruit trees and bushes. Ensure that the soil contains plenty of organic matter and stake them firmly so that their roots are not disturbed by the trees rocking in strong winds.

Choosing plants

One of the most common concerns for any setting looking to begin growing plants with their children is to choose what to grow. The choice of available seeds, bulbs, plants and trees can seem daunting, particularly to the novice gardener. There are a number of factors that you might consider when visiting the garden centre for the first time and you will soon develop the confidence to try growing something new.

What conditions will you be growing in?

Although it is possible to create artificial conditions to suit most plants, it is far easier when you are starting out to choose plants that are more likely to thrive in the conditions you already have. You may have already tested your soil to identify pH and soil type (see the Getting Started chapter for more details on this)

and this will already give you some idea of plants to avoid. Think about where the plants will be situated – will they receive full sun or are they shaded by trees or buildings for most of the day? Remember to consider the expected height of adjacent plants as this can create shade not present when you are initially planting. How windy is your plot? If you are planning to plant tall crops such as sunflowers or runner beans they will need staking and strong winds can soon cause damage as the plants grow.

Also, consider the extent to which your plants will be exposed to frost damage. If you live in the warmer South of the UK, you may feel confident that the risk of frost has past by early May, whereas further north, late frosts can create havoc to new growth. Few settings have the luxury of a polytunnel or greenhouse which can be used to raise the temperature allowing you to start the growing season earlier and continue it well into the autumn. However a simple cloche can be constructed from plastic tubing and clear plastic sheeting – just take a look on the internet for cheap ways to give young plants protection from the cold.

Are you looking for permanent or seasonal plants?

You may have areas within your garden which you wish to plant with hardy perennials or shrubs for a more permanent display. This might include a sensory area, herb garden or flower bed close to your entrance. Once again the children can be involved in choosing and maintaining the plants and will develop a good understanding of the needs of the plants throughout the season. However, ensure that you leave areas for planting year on year so that each new group of children can experience the delight of seeing something grow from seed. It is not necessary to set aside a huge area as even a couple of attractive containers or growbags should be sufficient.

Do you have time restrictions?

Some settings such as schools can be challenged by the need to fit in with holidays when the garden may have to be left to fend for itself. Even if this is not the case, you may have a group of children for a limited time and need to plan so that they can experience the whole process of seed to plate. If growing fruit or vegetables, choose those which will be ready for harvesting earlier in the year. There are many different varieties available but some to look out for include:

- Broad beans: Dwarf varieties tend to be hardier than those which grow taller – try The Sutton and Claudia Aquadulce which will not need staking.

- Berries: Choose plants with an early fruiting time - strawberries such as Mae can be planted up in a hanging basket or pot and kept indoors somewhere cool until placing outside in April for an earlier crop. Raspberry Glen Moy fruits throughout June and July.

- Carrots: Napoli, Early Nantes and Adelaide should be ready for harvesting in June or July.

- Peas: For tasty, early peas, try Early Onward which can be planted from February.

- Potatoes: Good early varieties to choose include Swift and Rocket.

- Rhubarb: By keeping your rhubarb plants in the dark with an upturned bucket in January and early February, you will soon get delicious slim, pale pink stems.

- Shallots: These onion-like bulbs are easy to grow – choose Longor or Golden Gourmet for planting in February.

Where possible, warm the soil first using heavy-duty polythene cloches. Many crops are quick to mature which is especially important with young children who can soon become frustrated if there is little to show for their hard work. Radishes are ready to eat only three or four weeks after sowing and can be sown regularly for a continuous crop.

A heated propagator can be purchased relatively cheaply and will allow you to sow your seeds earlier in the season. Alternatively, make use of a sunny window ledge to germinate seeds in a frost-free environment. It is not essential to grow plants from seed as most can be bought as seedling or plug plants (small plants with established roots). Garden centres and nurseries will have a wide range of flowering plants and vegetables which can be purchased while they are small before growing them on. This may give you a higher success rate but remember that the children will not have seen the complete process so balance this approach with sowing hardy seeds directly outdoors.

Suitable plants for children

When selecting plants for your garden there are some that you will wish to avoid. Obviously you would not choose plants known to be poisonous if eaten or those which may cause an allergic reaction if crushed on the skin. These are discussed in more detail in the Staying safe chapter. However, you may also need to consider whether to include any plants which have prickles or those which could sting. Some settings decide that it is better to avoid any plants with potential risks whereas others will use the opportunity to show children how to take care in the garden.

What appeals to children?

When planning what to grow, involve the children in the making the selection. Seed catalogues generally have brightly coloured pictures which can inspire children to think about what they could choose. Bring in a selection of edible foods and think about those which can be grown in our climate. Use this as an opportunity to discuss which ones they prefer to eat as these will generally be the first varieties to try. You might even keep a record of those foods they are prepared to taste and compare this to their reactions when trying home-grown produce. Many children will enjoy fruit or vegetables gathered and washed straight from their garden which they would not consider from the supermarket packet.

Young children are usually attracted to brightly coloured flowers and fruit and this can be an appealing place to start. However, they will equally be fascinated by plants which stimulate the senses such as the soft suede-like leaves of the Lamb's Ear (*Stachys Byzantina*) or the strongly scented Curry Plant (*Helichrysum Italicum*). Search out unusual varieties of common vegetables such as round carrots (such as Thumberline or Mini Round) or black tomatoes (Black Cherry).

Do you want a themed garden?

It can be fun to create a small area of garden with a specific theme. This can be used to stimulate imaginative play or could link to a particular story or topic you are focusing on. Themed gardens may require the introduction of plants chosen to create a particular environment which might not naturally thrive in our climate or in the conditions found in your garden. To ensure that the garden remains healthy, it is not necessary to replicate the plants which would naturally occur in that environment, but instead choose those which create the feeling of the place. Here are some suggestions for themed gardens. But remember, this is an opportunity to bring far off or imaginary lands into your settings, so be creative!

Jungle

Introduce a jungle into the corner of your garden and you can be sure that lions will be visiting before you know it. These plants need somewhere hot, so choose a sunny corner and be prepared to give the plants some additional protection with garden fleece in the winter. If you wish to add fencing to the area, it is possible to buy rolls of screening made from reed or bamboo relatively cheaply. Tropical plants have adapted to leaving in hot environments – for example succulents have a waxy coating which helps to prevent the loss of water. Many have silver or grey leaves to reflect the heat such as globe artichokes and some have spiky leaves to cut down on loss of water through a reduced surface area. Be careful where you include plants with sharp spikes though, as they could easily injure a child.

Plants you may wish to include are:

- *Gunnera Manicata*

- Cordyline

- Cardoon

- Hardy Banana

- Ornamental grasses

- Ferns

- Hostas

Desert

It is possible to create an arid, desert-looking garden if plants are chosen with care. Obviously, the further south you are based, the easier it will be to ensure the success of your garden but the most important starting point is a south-facing, preferably sloping site with sandy, well drained soil. Organic matter can be used to improve the drainage of heavy soils and the addition of large quantities of grit will prevent the plant roots from becoming water-logged. Space the plants well and sink rocks into the ground for added interest. The area can be mulched with gravel, which will protect the plants and reduce the amount of weeding required.

This style of garden would be perfect for small world play and perhaps children could be encouraged to build small nomad tents from lolly sticks and lightweight cotton material.

Suitable plants include:

■ *Aloes*

■ *Agaves*

■ *Echiums*

■ *Echinopsis*

Fairy woodland

It is easier to create a magical woodland if you have an area of existing trees which provide shade. Think about planting bulbs and shade-loving perennials under the canopy of trees to add interest throughout the year. Make somewhere to sit using sections of different sized logs or look for hand-carved wooden mushrooms and use chipped bark to mark out paths

and clearings. It is now possible to buy resin features which can be attached to the trunk of a tree to create faces or alternatively children can form their own from modelling material. Storytelling can help to bring the area to life, and children could have access to some fancy dress costumes or make their own fairy crowns from willow withies and hedgerow leaves. Sticks can soon be transformed into wands with the addition of feathers and ribbons and fairies can be made from old wooden pegs with scraps of material attached.

Plants to include might be:

■ Bluebells

■ Wood Anemones

■ Primroses

■ Cowslips

■ *Cyclamen*

■ Snowdrops

■ Ferns

■ Honeysuckle

Keeping records

Do not forget to document your garden successes and failures as you go along. Involve the children in creating journals or displays detailing what they have grown and when. They can be responsible for weighing or measuring their produce allowing you to compare year on year. You might like to use digital cameras to record the different stages of growth which you can they revisit at different stages throughout the season. These pictures can also be displayed allowing visitors to see how the garden has grown.

Reading packets and labels

When buying seed or plants you will usually be presented with a certain amount of valuable information. This will generally include both the common and botanical names and further instructions on how and where to grow. Often the information can be hard to understand as it may be a mixture of text, charts and symbols. The diagram on the following page shows some of the features to look out for but, if in doubt, find a knowledgeable person in your garden centre or nursery to help you understand whether it is best suited to your needs.

What to look for on a seed packet

Gives you some idea of how many seeds the packet contains and whether it is good value for money

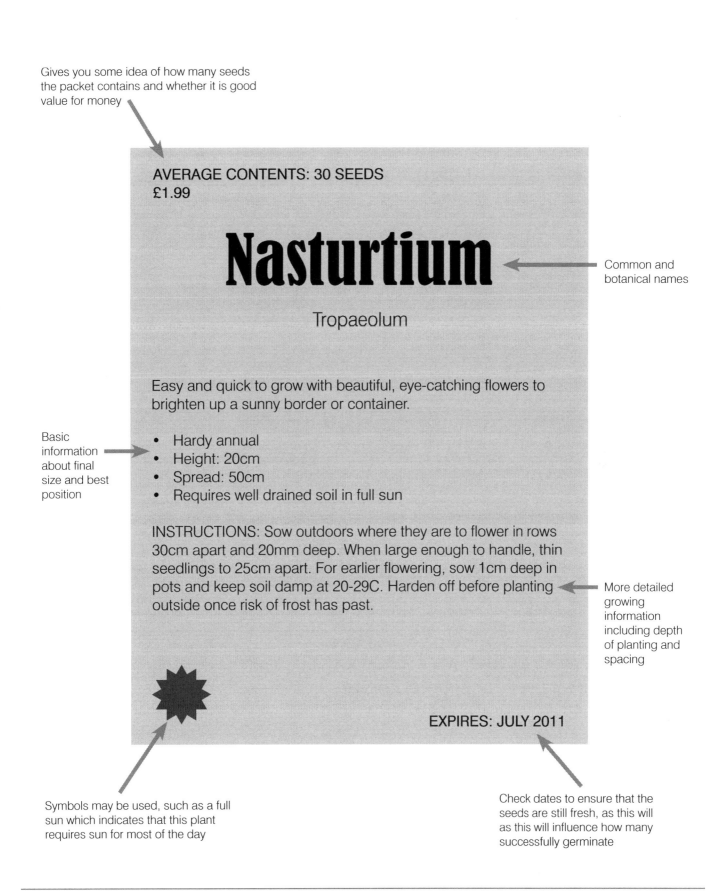

AVERAGE CONTENTS: 30 SEEDS
£1.99

Nasturtium

Tropaeolum

Common and botanical names

Easy and quick to grow with beautiful, eye-catching flowers to brighten up a sunny border or container.

Basic information about final size and best position

- Hardy annual
- Height: 20cm
- Spread: 50cm
- Requires well drained soil in full sun

INSTRUCTIONS: Sow outdoors where they are to flower in rows 30cm apart and 20mm deep. When large enough to handle, thin seedlings to 25cm apart. For earlier flowering, sow 1cm deep in pots and keep soil damp at 20-29C. Harden off before planting outside once risk of frost has past.

More detailed growing information including depth of planting and spacing

EXPIRES: JULY 2011

Symbols may be used, such as a full sun which indicates that this plant requires sun for most of the day

Check dates to ensure that the seeds are still fresh, as this will as this will influence how many successfully germinate

Planting calendar

Name of plant	Where to sow	When to sow	When to harvest	Helpful information
Garlic	Plant individual cloves directly outdoors	January to February	July onwards when the leaves start to yellow	Plant about 5-10cm deep allowing 20cm between plants
Tomato	Indoors in trays, then transplant to pots	March to April	July to October	Plant outside when the risk of frost has passed. Stake as they grow and remove side shoots so there is one male stem. Feed regularly. Do not attempt to grow if you cannot care for the plants over the summer.
Cornflower	Indoors into modular trays	March to April		
Carrot	Directly outdoors	End of March or April	June-July	If you have heavy, clay soil, try round carrots instead. Plant thin seedlings about 5cm apart. Plant strong smelling plants nearby, such as onions to help prevent carrot root fly.
Lettuce	Indoors in trays or outside when warmer	March to April indoors; or late May outdoors	From June onwards	To avoid pests, sow indoors and then plant outside when risk of frost has passed. Sow regularly to ensure a regular supply. Experiment with different varieties, such as rocket and Mizuna.
Mangetout peas	Directly outdoors	Late March to April	June to July, when pods are about 5cm long	Allow 5cm between seeds and at least 40cm between rows. Give support with string, netting or sticks as they grow.
Potato	Directly outdoors in rich soil	Late March to April (earliest) or mid April to May (maincrop)	June onwards when foliage begins to die back	By chitting the potatoes first, they will mature more quickly. Place somewhere light until they sprout and plant when shoots are about 2.5cm long. Plant early potatoes at least 10cm deep and the maincrop at least 15cm deep. As the foliage grows 'earth up' by covering the shoots with soil from nearby on a regular basis.
Spring onion	Sow outdoors thinly	End of March	June to July	Can be planted in small spaces and harvested before surrounding crops grow larger.
Runner bean	Individually in pots indoor	April	Late June to August	Plant outside after risk of frost has passed, allowing 15cm between plants. Support with a wigwam of canes or netting.

Name of plant	Where to sow	When to sow	When to harvest	Helpful information
French bean	Indoors in pots	Mid April	July	To avoid damage by slugs or birds grow indoors in pots and plant outside when 10cm tall. If using climbing plants they will need a wigwam for support.
Courgette	Indoors, individually in pots	Mid to late April	July onwards – pick before they get too big	Plant outside after risk of frost has gone, spacing about 60cm apart.
Nasturtium	Indoors or outdoors	April to May		The leaves are edible and have a slightly peppery taste when added to salads
Poached egg plant	Directly outdoors	Late April to May		Shade-tolerant and will encourage bees.
Sweetcorn	Indoors in pots	Late April	July to September	Plant outdoors in large blocks in late May allowing 50cm between plants. Press the corn to see if it is ripe; it will ooze a creamy liquid when ready for harvesting.
Sunflower	Indoors in pots	Mid April to May		Plant outside at the end of May. Support as they grow and leave the seeds to feed the birds in the Autumn.
English marigold	Outdoors into the soil	Late April to May		Also known as the pot marigold.
Radish	Outdoors thinly into soil	April to May	May to June	Plant 2.5cm apart. Radishes will mature in three to four weeks.
Strawberry	Outdoors in full sunshine and well-drained soil	Plant runners late in Autumn or early Spring	Late May to July	Replace plants with new runners every three years.
Pumpkin/ Squash	Indoors individually in pots	Mid April to May	September to October	Plant outside in late May to June allowing at least 1m between plants.
Poppy	Outdoors where they are to flower	May		Will self-seed freely.
Broad bean	Directly outdoors	Autumn or early Spring	When the pods are 6cm long	Plant 15cm apart and pinch off the tops of the plants when the first pods appear. Susceptible to blackfly; can be controlled by regular spraying with a weak solution of washing up liquid.
Onion sets	Straight in to the ground	October to November	June to July as required	Plant 15cm apart so that the pointed end is on the top and just visible. They like fertile but not newly composted soil.

What resources do we need?

Once you have finished the hard landscaping of your new garden and started to think about what you wish to grow in it, you will need to collect together some additional resources before you can start using it. It is not necessary to spend huge amounts of money; with a little bit of ingenuity and persuasion, you can often acquire a range of useful items to support your gardening activities. Without suitable equipment, the children and staff will become frustrated and despondent, so regularly monitor that you have enough equipment and check that it remains in good condition.

Home links

Parents are often concerned about their children's clothes becoming dirty while taking part in gardening activities. Encourage them to send their children in old clothes that are ok to get dirty and muddy, or ask parents to send a spare set of outdoor clothing for them to use when they are gardening.

Storage

You may need to invest in some secure storage for equipment, such as tools, pots and spare seeds. Garden sheds are affordable and easy to install. They come in many shapes and sizes; it is worth investing in the largest you can accommodate as it can be extremely frustrating trying to organize equipment with restricted room. Consider whether a window is necessary to provide light and if you need to add wall shelves or a work bench. Most sheds are constructed from wood, metal or plastic. Wooden sheds can look most attractive but be aware of the different methods of timber construction as this will influence both price and durability. Metal sheds are generally strong and secure and can be painted to make them more appealing. If you do not require much storage space, consider a plastic shed. They are affordable, hard-wearing and the lightest option, so they are easier to reposition if necessary.

Ensure that your storage is placed close to your growing area. The children will need to take responsibility for the gardening equipment so allow them to enter the storage space and use pictures to mark shelves and hooks to help them to correctly return items after use.

Clothing

If the children are to feel happy and confident taking part in gardening activities throughout the year, they need to have access to suitable clothing. In cold or wet weather they need warm coats or raincoats and on sunny days sunhats will help to protect them from overexposure to the sun.

When gardening, the children's needs might be slightly different to when generally playing outdoors. They will need to be able to move freely, often kneeling or sitting on the ground. Footwear is also important as they may be walking on muddy or wet ground. A selection of spare Wellington boots should be available for when children do not have their own (these can be obtained through donations or from charity shops). Consider purchasing salopettes or all-in-ones to ensure that all children can enjoy the garden without worrying about staying clean or comfortable.

There is often a debate over whether it is necessary to provide gloves to children when involved in gardening activities.

Children's gardening gloves can be hard to find, particularly in small sizes. Many adults complain that it is hard to carry out gardening tasks when wearing gloves and most children find it hard to use tools while wearing gloves. The argument against wearing gloves is that children need direct contact with the natural world; something that many children are no longer exposed to and is one of the special features of gardening. Maintain simple procedures to reduce the chances of infection from the soil, such as regularly checking the garden for animal faeces, covering children's cuts or grazes and ensuring that a rigorous hand-washing routine is in place.

Tools

There are a wide range of tools and equipment that you will need as the garden develops. You may be fortunate to receive donations from supportive gardeners, but you will probably need to purchase a range of child-appropriate tools. Below are suggestions for what you might want to collect for your gardening toolkit.

- Hand forks and hand trowels: it is worth investing in good-quality tools that will last for more than one season. There are a number of companies that supply tools designed especially for children; visiting a local garden centre should also give you some idea of what is available. Ensure that you have enough forks and trowels for children to use while

working in groups; as they can become frustrated if they are made to wait for another child to finish.

- Long-handled tools: these include spades, forks, rakes, brooms, and hoes. Look for well-made children's versions; not toys.

- Watering cans: watering the plants is often the children's favourite activity. Buy plenty of watering cans that are small and light enough to carry when full of water.

- Wheelbarrows.

- Secateurs: these are for adult use only. Find some way of attaching them by cord to your clothing, as it is very easy to become distracted and put them down.

- Kneeling mats: these are cheap and easy to find. They help to keep the children's clothes clean and make kneeling down much more comfortable.

- Flower pots and seed trays: plastic pots will hold moisture for longer but terracotta pots generally look better.

- Potting compost for containers: choose peat-free multipurpose compost for most activities.

- Plant labels, twine, garden canes or hazel sticks, netting.

Containers

Containers can add interest to even the smallest garden and are invaluable where money is in short supply. They can also be use creatively to enhance small spaces, perhaps around an entrance way, or on an uninspiring wall.

Always clean the container thoroughly before it is used to ensure that it is free from pests and diseases. Ensure that water can drain freely by making several holes in the bottom if not already present and prevent these from getting clogged up by covering with a layer of broken pots or stones. Fill the container with organic, peat-free compost ready for planting. Free standing containers tend to dry out more quickly than beds. You can reduce the water loss by lining the container with cardboard or old woollen jumpers. You might also consider adding water-storing gels or granules to the compost which will help hold moisture for longer.

Containers are ideally suited to planting bedding plants or vegetables which can then be removed at the end of the season. Generally, the bigger the plants when mature, the larger the container it will require. However, plants in containers look better when grown more closely together so that there are not too many spaces between them. You will find a wide range of colourful bedding plants suitable for container growing at your local garden centre and you could choose to grow them from seeds, plugs (young plants) or the more expensive option of buying mature plants. Almost any vegetable can be grown in a container but you should look for miniature or "baby" varieties. For example, you could try small tomatoes such as Tumbling Tom or round carrots such as Mini Round.

Do not feel that you have to settle for a pot from the garden centre – visit the local municipal tip or boot sale, ask parents for donations and involve the children in choosing appropriate plants for a range of unusual containers. Some ideas for inspiration include:

Tyres

Tyres can be used as a cheap and flexible container for many types of plant. They are readily available from garages as they have to pay for disposing old tyres. Clean them thoroughly to remove any grease or oil before painting. Use vinyl silk emulsion paint as this is washable when wet but dries to provide a good finish which will gradually fade over time. Tyres can be stacked on top of each other and industrial spray adhesive used if you wish to permanently attach them. They can also successfully be used to grow potatoes. Add further tyres and organic matter to cover the tops of the plants as they appear.

Wellington boots

Wellies and other large boots such as colourful Doc Martens make fun containers for growing flowering plants and herbs.

Old ceramic sinks

Sinks have traditionally been used for planting alpines. Several years ago, people started covering them with hypertufa, made from cement and peat, to give the illusion of real stone but they can be just as attractive left uncovered.

Window boxes

These can be readily bought from the garden centre or perhaps you have a parent with good carpentry skills who could build some for you. Beware of attaching anything to the wall at a height where a child might knock their head and ensure that all fixings are secure.

Large catering cans

Old canteen sized catering cans or cooking oil tins make attractive and interesting growing containers. Once again, ensure that you have allowed for good drainage.

Hanging baskets

These are a simple way to add interest to a boring wall. It is possible to buy wire baskets which will need lining with ready-made liners or moss collected from your garden, and more naturalistic woven baskets which are normally only planted from the top. You might also add slow release plant food as the compost in hanging baskets soon becomes stripped of its nutrients and the plants will require regular feeding for maximum growth and flowers.

Wooden wine boxes

Wine boxes and crates can make a colourful display if lined with plastic and then planted with a range of annuals. They may not last for more than a single year but this should not be a concern if you are able to obtain them from a local wine merchant free of charge.

Grow bags

Growing bags are ideal where you do not have permanent beds and since they are only used for one season, the compost should be free from disease and full of nutrients. They are ideal for growing up to three vegetable plants and are best suited for those which do not have deep roots such as tomatoes, peppers, aubergines and courgettes. Position in a sunny spot and pierce the plastic to give drainage. Most are pre-marked to show you where to cut the bag when planting. Tall growing crops will need to be staked and it is possible to buy a frame to support the canes which can be inserted beside the plants.

Old baskets

These will rot eventually but look beautiful planted with a range of herbs.

Chimney pots

A traditional idea, but old terracotta pots are becoming increasingly hard to find as people recognise their value as an interesting garden ornament.

Food packaging

A fun project is to see how many plants you can successfully grow using relevant food packaging as containers. For example try growing a single potato in a large crisp packet, or wheat in a cereal box which comes with its own waterproof liner.

Caring for the plants

This section focuses on the most common techniques required when gardening which have been simplified, where possible, for the younger gardener. The inexperienced adult gardener will sometimes find it easier to work with young children in the garden because he/she will share the challenge of trying out new skills for the first time. 'New' gardeners are less likely to make assumptions about how children should tackle a task.

Sowing seeds

If you are sowing seeds into pots or seed/module trays, select suitable peat-free compost and ensure that it does not contain any sizable lumps. When sowing seeds directly outside in the garden, prepare the soil so that any stones, lumps or weeds are removed. You can do this with a rake, or by crumbling the soil between your fingers as when making pastry. If you have particularly stony soil, use a sieve to remove anything that may get in the way of the young seedlings. This activity is a good opportunity for teamwork with a small group of children, working together to fill and then shake the sieve.

Sowing seeds can be a tricky task, especially for very young children. It is often easier to sprinkle the seeds if they are tipped into the palm of one hand, and the thumb and forefinger of the other hand are used to pinch a few before releasing them gradually into place. The children can practise this technique using sand. Draw a shape or letter into the soil with a stick and see if the children can cover it with a fine sprinkling of sand. When sowing the actual seeds, you can mix them with a little sand to ensure that they are spread more thinly over the soil. Always keep hold of the seed packet otherwise hundreds of tiny seeds may soon be accidently tipped out onto the ground. Some seeds, especially those with a hard outside coating, such as sweet peas, benefit from being soaked in warm water overnight before planting. Larger seeds are easier to handle and can be sown individually in small pots. Remember to label pots immediately, particularly if you are sowing more than one type of seed in a session.

Ensure that the soil is flat before you start sowing and follow the instructions on the back of the seed pack to gauge spacing and depth of sowing. Generally, seeds need to be sown twice

as deep as the smallest seed's diameter. Water them sparingly after sowing using a watering can with a fine rose head. If you are sowing into trays, placing clingfilm over the trays creates warm and damp conditions that are ideal for germination. Remove the clingfilm as soon as the seedlings appear to avoid 'damping off', a fungal infection that can quickly wipe out a whole tray of young plants. Keep the trays somewhere warm or use a heated propagator for the first couple of weeks.

Planting

There are a few simple rules that the children should be taught to follow when planting.

- When digging a plant out of the ground, loosen the soil around the roots and try to lift the plant out, disturbing the roots as little as possible.

- To loosen a plant from a pot, turn the pot upside down and squeeze it gently a few times to release the root ball.

- When replanting, try to ensure that the plant is at the same level in the soil as before, with the roots covered.

- If planting in a container, avoid filling the soil right to the top, or the soil will be washed over the edge when it is watered.

- Water plants regularly until they have established and no longer show any signs of wilting.

It is a good idea to plant bulbs to bring colour to pots and borders early in the season, before much else is growing. Hardy bulbs, such as crocuses, daffodils and tulips can be planted in the autumn and if left outside, should begin to flower the following spring. If they are planted in containers, make sure that they do not become waterlogged as this can lead to rotting. Rotting can be prevented by adding a layer of stones at the bottom of a pot. Talk to the children about the importance

of planting the bulbs the right way up, with the more pointed end facing upwards and the more rounded end, which may be showing signs of roots, at the bottom. Follow the instructions on the packet to ensure they are planted at the right depth.

Thinning

'Thinning' is the process that reduces the number of seedlings, allowing more space for the others to grow into strong and healthy plants. Select the weaker looking seedlings and either gently remove or snip off the growth. It is a hard lesson to teach children as you have to be ruthless; if you are thinning salad vegetables, offer the baby plants to the children as a tasty snack.

Pricking out, potting on and planting out

'Pricking out' is the process of moving seedlings into a larger container. Wait until two leaves have grown and use a pencil to loosen the soil around the roots. Lift the seedlings by the leaves and gently reposition them into ready-prepared holes before firming the soil and watering.

Most seedlings will survive 'pricking out' without any ill effects, but some dislike being moved and need to be planted where they are to eventually grow. You should be able to find this information on the back of the seed packet. One way to minimize the disturbance is by planting some crops in toilet rolls filled with compost; these can later be planted directly into the ground (the cardboard of the toilet roll will eventually rot). This technique works particularly well for carrots, sweet peas and beans.

'Potting on' is the process of moving small plants into larger pots where they can continue to develop. They will already have formed a healthy root system and now require more room.

'Planting out' refers to the stage when your plants are ready to go outside and they have been hardened off (see below).

Before planting out, ensure that they have been well watered an hour or two in advance. For a thorough soaking, consider putting them in a container of water so that it soaks up into the compost from below. Involve the children in digging a hole before releasing a plant from its pot. If you have another pot of the same size, this can be used to check that the hole in the ground is deep enough. Once the plant is in position, firm the soil and give it another generous watering.

Hardening off

Plants that have been started life indoors will need a period of time to acclimatize to the often cooler outdoor weather. Start by placing them outside during the day. If you have a sheltered spot, they can be left out overnight but be prepared to bring them in if a late frost is forecast. Encourage the children to monitor the outdoor temperature using a maximum and minimum thermometer.

Watering

When gardening, children love to water! They love it so much that it is easy to wash seeds away or swamp young plants before they have a chance to get established. It is also easy for the soil to quickly dry out and so organizing a good watering schedule may be one of the most important factors for a successful garden.

The frequency of how often you need to water the garden will depend upon many factors, such as the weather and the extent to which the soil retains water. For example, the soil in a container will generally dry out more quickly than the soil in a flowerbed. Water plants at the start or end of the day; this will ensure that the water evaporates slowly and will prevent plants from becoming scorched in hot weather. Regular watering will allow your plants to develop a healthy root system.

Weeding and mulching

A 'weed' is simply a plant that grows where it is not supposed to. One of the greatest challenges for a novice gardener is the ability to identify what is a weed and what is simply a seedling of something sown intentionally. Regular weeding is essential to prevent your plot from disappearing under a carpet of fast-growing annual weeds.

Show the children how to use a hoe during the weeding process. Run the hoe over the soil to cut off the green shoots of the weeds; these can be left to wilt or can be picked out by hand. This is a quick and easy method but the children will need to be sure of which plants to hoe and which to leave alone. When involving children in weeding, it works better in areas of the garden that are well established, such as around strawberry

or tomato plants. Alternatively, children will love the chance to weed by hand. One of the safest ways to do this is to give each child a weed and ask them to see how many more of the same they can find. You could introduce a challenge of who can find the tallest weed or the one with the longest roots.

'Mulch' is spread on the surface of the soil to suppress the growth of weeds. It also conservese moisture, protects the roots and feeds the plants. Many organic and inorganic materials can be use to make 'mulch'; consider which materials are most appropriate to use when making mulch with young children.

Garden compost and bark chippings are ideal. Cocoa shells can be used and they have a fantastic chocolate smell (but they can be harmful to dogs who are attracted to eat them, causing severe irritation to their digestive systems). Well-rotted horse or cow manure makes excellent mulch, which will greatly improve the structure of the soil, but it may not be suitable to use around young children (unless you follow very careful and thorough hand-washing routines). Restrict the use of mulch to the autumn, when it can be spread over the ground and left untouched over the winter to be drawn down into the soil by worms.

Feeding

All plants need a good supply of nutrients, such as potassium to promote flowering, fruiting and leaf growth; and phosphorous to stimulate root growth. These nutrients can be provided to plants by supplying additional feed when required. (If you have time to produce rich, good-quality soil, then there will be less of a need to give additional feeds through the growing season.) Follow the feeding guidelines below:

■ Use a liquid feed on a weekly basis for flowering plants in pots and hanging baskets. Alternatively, use controlled-release fertiliser granules or plugs pushed into the compost to deliver a supply of nutrients through the summer.

■ Provide vegetables with slow-release fertilisers several times throughout the growing season.

■ Flowerbeds and borders will benefit from a covering of slow-release fertiliser in the spring, known as 'top dressing'.

Pruning

'Pruning' is sometimes necessary to promote the development of fruit or flowers. It may also be required to stop larger shrubs or trees from becoming leggy or too big for their surroundings. Knowing how and when to carry out 'pruning' can be rather daunting at first. Below are some general tips but for more specific advice check the plant label, consult a specialist book or seek out an enthusiastic gardener!

■ Start by removing unwanted growth, which is either dead, diseased or in the wrong place.

■ Use sharp secateurs to make a clean diagonal cut directly above an outward facing bud or side shoot.

■ Regular deadheading of flowering annuals will encourage further flowers to form.

■ Pinch out the growing tip of annuals to encourage the side shoots to make a bushier plant.

■ Encourage flowering perennials to produce further flowers by giving them a gentle trim once the initial flowers begin to fade.

Harvesting

Try to harvest crops when they are at their best. This may mean that you have a huge glut of a particular vegetable and on other occasions your harvest might be frustratingly small and difficult to share fairly with a group of enthusiastic 'taste' volunteers. Depending on the crop, there are many different ways to gather in the harvest. Vegetables growing underground will need gentle exploration to ensure that they are ready. Radishes and baby carrots can be easily pulled out of the ground by the children, whereas others, such as potatoes and onions, will require the soil to be carefully loosened with a garden fork. Other crops can be gathered directly from the plant, such as beans or tomatoes. These can be snapped off or snipped with a pair of scissors. Show the children what a ripe example looks like so that the plants are not stripped of their entire growth.

Some of your harvest produce is likely to make it off the plant and straight into young mouths. The remaining produce can be used in cooking or shared with the local community. Crops that store well, such as onions and garlic can be cleaned and dried out in a cool dark space.

Caring for the environment

Involving children in growing creates an ideal opportunity to introduce them to many environmental issues. There is evidence to suggest that this will increase the likelihood of them being more sensitive to the needs of the environment as they get older. There are many ways in which you can create a garden without impacting adversely upon the planet and you may find that your plants reward you with greater and stronger growth.

Dealing with pests

Sooner or later you are going to find that something you have grown has been eaten, damaged or completely wiped out by pests. If this has been caused by birds or mammals such as squirrels, cats or mice, then you will firstly have the challenge of keeping them away from your crops in the future. The most effective way may be to create a physical barrier where possible, such as fencing or netting. You could also try repellents such as those containing pepper powder which will need regularly reapplying, or an electronic device which works by emitting an ultrasonic sound triggered by a motion sensor.

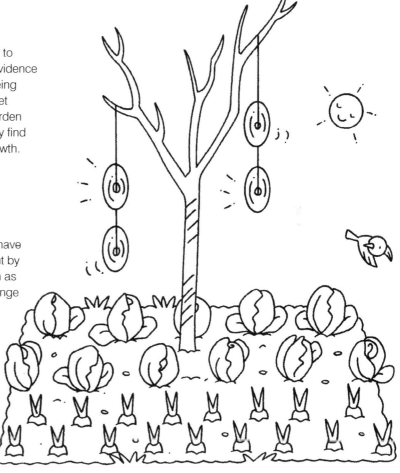

Alternatively, it may be a thriving insect population that is responsible for the destruction. It may be tempting to reach for a pesticide but this should be avoided for many reasons.

▪ Pesticides are poisons and are therefore unsuitable to use around small children.

▪ They often kill the good bugs as well as the unwanted bugs.

▪ Other birds and animals can suffer if they eat insects poisoned by pesticides.

There are many safer and more environmentally friendly options such as:

▪ Remove slugs and caterpillars by hand.

▪ Use a solution of diluted washing up liquids to spray on aphids.

▪ Collect and crush eggshells to sprinkle around delicate plants such as lettuces to deter slugs and snails.

▪ Build a scarecrow or use old CDs suspended from string so that they glint in the light detracting birds.

▪ A child's windmill stuck in the ground is supposed to scare away moles. Alternatively bury a musical birthday card as they will be driven away by the sound.

Positioning certain plants close to others can have a natural beneficial effect on reducing the number of unwanted pests and diseases. Different plants attract particular insects which may in turn feed upon those bugs you are trying to discourage. This is known as companion planting. For example, growing onions and carrots together can help to keep away carrot fly which is fooled by the strong smell of the onions. French marigolds produce a pesticidal chemical from their roots which can work against the potato eel worm. Plant basil near to tomatoes as it attracts aphids to it and they are more likely to leave the tomatoes alone.

Another way to prevent the build up of pests and diseases in the soil is to follow the principles of crop rotation. This also evens out the demands of the plants on the soil as different crops take up different levels of nutrients. A simple system is not to grow the same crops in the same place for two years running. Vegetables fall into different categories (see table 1 below) and to maximise the benefits of crop rotation you may wish to follow a four year cycle as suggested in table 2. This example of cross rotation involves dividing your growing space into four equal-sized areas and planning to grow crops from each category in a different area each year. Choose crops to grow from each of the four categories below. Now divide your growing space into four equal-sized areas.

Table 1: Categories of vegetables

Root crops	Brassicas	Onions and Legumes	Potato family
Carrots Beetroot Parsnip Celery	Cabbage Cauliflower Brussels sprouts Broccoli Turnips Swede Radish	Onions Shallots Leeks Garlic Spring onions Broad beans Early pea Mangetout French beans Runner beans	Potatoes Tomatoes

Table 2: Four year cycle of crop rotation

	1st year	2nd year	3rd year	4th year
Area 1	Roots	Potatoes	Onions and Legumes	Brassicas
Area 2	Brassicas	Roots	Potatoes	Onions and Legumes
Area 3	Onions and Legumes	Brassicas	Roots	Potatoes
Area 4	Potatoes	Onions and Legumes	Brassicas	Roots

Conserving water

All plants require water but as a limited natural resource, it is important to show children ways in which you can reduce and recycle the water which you use. A water butt is an effective way to collect rainwater to keep plants watered. Rain can be directed off the roof of a building or shed by the means of guttering and into a carefully positioned container. Ensure that it has a lid which can be safely secured and a tap which the children can reach to fill their watering cans. You may also be able to recycle water from a water tray, or 'grey water' such as that used in washing up. Encourage the children to come up with ingenious ways to transport it to the garden, maybe using buckets or a system constructed from guttering.

Spreading a thick mulch onto the soil will help to reduce evaporation and reduce the frequency that you need to water. Try to encourage the children to water only the roots and not the foliage, the adjacent soil and their feet!

Some plants are more drought-tolerant than others so you might wish to use these in your garden. Choose plants which would naturally receive less water such as those grown in the hot Mediterranean. This will in turn increase their chances of survival if they need to be left unwatered over the summer period. Some recommended drought-tolerant plants include:

- *Achillea*

- Cabbage tree (*Cordyline*)

- *Geranium*

- *Potentilla*

- Lavender

- Sea Pink

- *Santolina*

Composting

It is a good idea to create a compost area within your garden fairly early on in your project. This will mean that not only will you have somewhere to dispose of much of your unwanted garden waste, but it will also allow maximum time for the compost to form. Adding compost to your soil, either as a mulch or mixed in, will improve its structure and act as the ultimate slow release garden fertiliser. Healthy compost requires a balance of green materials, brown materials, water and air. Below are some examples of what should and should not be added.

Green materials include:

- Fruit and vegetable peelings from snack time

- Tea bags or coffee granules

- Crushed egg shells

- Dead flowers

- Grass cuttings (but use sparingly)

Brown materials include:

- Small twigs

- Leaves

- Scrunched up cardboard & paper

- Straw

- Sawdust

Avoid:

- Cooked food

- Dog or cat faeces

- Weeds or diseased plants

- Shiny paper

- Nappies

It is possible to purchase a readymade composting bin and some settings may be fortunate to have one donated. Alternatively you can create your own heap, using wooden planks, wire netting or old pallets to contain the compost material. Position your compost bin directly onto the soil as this will allow worms to travel up from the earth below. Add small layers of alternate brown and green waste being careful never to add too much of a single material in one go. Keep the heap moist but not too wet and try to turn it each week to add air. This can be virtually impossible though if you have one of the modern 'dalek-style' bins. You should soon notice that the compost is beginning to warm up. At no time should it smell of anything other than healthy soil. If it does, try to turn it more regularly and watch the balance of what you are adding. The compost should be ready between a few months and a year when it starts to have a crumbly texture and most of the materials are no longer distinguishable.

Home links

Organise a day when the children bring in a picnic lunch. Look to see how much of the leftover food and packaging can be added to the compost bin. Repeat a week later and this time challenge the parents and children to design a lunch in which all of the waste is compostable.

or a hanging mobile created from old metal cutlery attached to nylon thread. Perhaps children could be encouraged to bring in unwanted objects and work together to come up with creative solutions as to how they might be used. Points to consider when using recycled materials in the garden are:

- Art from recycled materials is not meant to be permanent so remember to change displays regularly to keep them looking fresh.

- Consider whether the items are environmentally friendly – will materials be a threat to wildlife?

- Aesthetics – settings sometimes worry that by using recycled materials their outdoor area will look 'untidy' and unprofessional. Educate parents and be sensitive to the outlook of neighbours.

- Weather-proof – your creations need to be rain-resistant so use acrylic paints rather than poster paints, and plastics rather than cardboard.

- Child-friendly – ensure that glues or paints are suitable for children. Have recycled materials been used to store washing powders or chemicals? Are tyres clean?

- Ensure that you recycle the materials appropriately once you have finished with them.

A fascinating addition to your garden is a wormery. It is possible to buy a kit (such as the one produce by Wiggly Wigglers) which includes everything you need to create a worm-assisted composting system. This will allow you to convert kitchen waste into rich compost and a concentrated liquid feed. A wormery requires simple upkeep, through regularly feeding cooked food scraps, vegetable peelings, tea leaves and shredded paper or cardboard to your worms and they will do the rest. The worms will gradually move into the next layer of your wormery allowing you access to the compost which is rich in nutrients and organic matter. Children will be intrigued by the process and will love to watch the worms at work.

Using recycled materials

Early years practitioners are usually very adept at using found or donated objects for a wide range of creative purposes and it is no different in the garden. Use your imagination to come up with alternative growing containers such as an old tin bath or toilet bowl. These can be decorated making an attractive talking point. Surfaces too need not always come from the builders' merchant. A collection of golf balls set in concrete makes a good if rather uneven path and broken crockery or bottle tops can be used to cover a wall, Gaudi-style. Consider adding sculptures made from recycled objects such as strips of plastic bag woven through the spokes of a bicycle wheel

Encouraging wildlife

An early years garden can provide a fantastic habitat for native species of insects, invertebrates, birds and small mammals. Although this can at times be in conflict with the desire to grow perfect, undamaged plants and produce, the benefits far outweigh the downside. To create an area of biodiversity (rich in living things), think about the habitats required by the species you are trying to attract.

- By introducing a range of different plants, you are providing animals with a source of plentiful food – fruits, leaves, seeds, pollen and nectar. Where possible try to select native plants which are more suited to the British climate. Some settings may wish to plant a butterfly border to encourage adult butterflies to visit, sucking up the nectar with their long tongue or probiscus. Position clumps of nectar-rich plants close together in a sunny, sheltered spot. Some plants that you may want to include are:

  - African Marigold

  - Butterfly Bush (*Buddleia Davidii*)

  - Catmint

  - Cornflower

  - Golden Rod

- Heather

- Lavender

- *Scabious*

- *Sedums*

- Stocks

- Sweet William

- Offer additional food throughout the winter such as nuts and seeds in a bird feeder. The children will be fascinated to see the many different visitors and will quickly become familiar with their names. They might even like to make their own bird food. Use a mixture of suet, seeds, breadcrumbs, and peanut butter to fill old yoghurt pots which can then be suspended upside down from the branches of a tree. Ensure that once you start to feed the birds, you continue well into the spring when sources of alternative food should increase. You can continue to put food out for the birds during the rest of the year, but ensure that you use a mesh feeder for peanuts which only allow small pieces to be taken, as whole peanuts could be harmful to young birds. A bowl of water will ensure that there is something to drink if there are no other water supplies such as a pond nearby. It may also encourage frogs and dragonflies.

- Plants and trees make excellent homes for a range of living things. Do not be too tidy at the end of the growing season and leave some plants undisturbed for insects to shelter in over the winter. Together with a pile of logs and leaves, this provides many animals with an ideal place to live.

- You may wish to create a 'meadow' area of wildflowers. This will work best in an area of grass where the fertility is low, so do not feed the grass and allow it to grow long. In the autumn, buy wildflowers as plug plants which can be inserted directly into the grass as this will help your meadow to establish itself more quickly. Plug plants are larger than seedlings and grow in trays containing lots of v-shaped cells to be planted directly into containers or soil. Good quality plugs should have green, healthy-looking leaves, and roots that are starting to appear at the bottom of each cell. Alternatively, buy wildflower turf which contains a mixture of half grasses and half native wildflowers, such as Yarrow and Ox-Eye Daisy. Cut the grass at the end of the summer when most of the flowers will have dropped their seeds, and then again in the spring. Always rake up the debris to prevent it from feeding the soil.

- Consider introducing a range of structures designed to offer shelter for wildlife such as bird boxes, hedgehog homes or insect houses. You might even build your own 'wildlife hotel' from a stack of old wooden

pallets filled with logs, lengths of bamboo, stones and leaves to create a diverse range of homes.

- The addition of a bog garden is often considered a safer and more manageable option than a pond. It is a patch of permanently wet ground which may encourage an abundance of interesting wildlife to visit such as dragonflies, frogs, toads and possibly even grass snakes. Either use an existing waterlogged depression, or dig out a shallow hole

and line with plastic or rubber pond liner. Pierce the liner at regular intervals and replace the soil, if possible adding some garden compost. Once the soil has settled, a variety of wildlife-friendly, native plants can be added such as:

- Ragged Robin

- Marsh Marigold

- *Iris Sibirica*

- Water Forget-me-not

- Bird's-Foot Trefoil

- *Primula Pulverulenta*

- Meadow Buttercup

- Scullcap

Staying safe

Gardening should be a safe and enjoyable experience. However, as with all activities, there are some basic health and safety issues to consider. Regular risk assessments should be normal practice within your setting and it is no different for the garden. You are looking to achieve a balance between creating an environment which provides the children with stimulation and new challenges, whilst removing potentially harmful hazards.

Following good practice

- Check the outside area first before allowing the children into the garden. Look out for rubbish which may have been left by unwanted visitors and also ensure that there has been no damage to any of the permanent features. Dog faeces should be removed as they can carry the harmful microorganism, *Toxocara Canis* which can lead to blindness. Cat faeces can also be harmful as it is possible to become infected with Toxoplasmosis, a parasitic disease.

- Store seed packets and bulbs safely. Children could be mistaken in thinking that bulbs are onions and might be tempted to have a taste but many bulbs can cause a severe reaction if eaten. Be watchful of young children when planting seeds and beans to ensure they do not put them in their mouths.

- Avoid using chemical products in the garden at all times and try to follow the principles of organic gardening instead.

- A number of rare but harmful diseases can be transmitted through soil, such as Weil's Disease which can enter the body through the skin. Develop a routine of always washing hands thoroughly after spending time in the garden. Invest in some nail brushes and show the children how they should be used. Cover cuts with plasters if allowed or supply the children with gardening gloves. Discourage children from putting their hands in their mouths unless they are clean.

- Tetanus spores can sometimes be present in the soil so again cover cuts and wash hands regularly. Importantly, try to ensure that children have received all their routine inoculations.

- Water is an endless source of fascination to children. However it is possible to drown in only a few centimetres of water so

ensure that children do not have unsupervised access at any time. Toddlers are most at risk as they are able to move around the garden but have yet to develop the coordination necessary to easily get out of water. Ponds should be securely fenced and/or covered and children shown the appropriate way to behave when they visit. A pebble fountain filled with large cobbles allows children to have safer access to water.

- Regularly check garden structures and surfaces for signs of wear and tear. Be alert to how different weather can affect them – paths can become very slippery in wet or icy weather.

- Teach children to behave appropriately around insects such as wasps and bees. Ensure that they can identify those insects which may be potentially harmful and model good behaviour yourself by not waving your arms around or running away!

- Stakes and canes may be used to support plants within the garden. However, unless they are very long, they can easily poke into the eyes of someone leaning over. Make the tops safe with either specially designed rubber caps or old, upended yoghurt pots.

- Ensure that garden twine or netting is not left somewhere where a small child could become entangled. Cut off any excess and fix down netting edges with plastic pegs.

Safe use of tools

When using tools, it is important that the children learn to handle them appropriately so as to minimise the possibility of accidents.

■ Ensure that children understand that tools are not toys to be played with and be watchful for inappropriate behaviour, particularly waving them around or using them as pretend weapons.

■ Avoid unnecessary risks by always storing tools securely.

■ First demonstrate how to use each tool correctly. You may need to repeat this each time the children are working in the garden.

■ Only allow children access to metal tools in the presence of an adult. You may wish to invest in some safer, plastic tools which the children can use as part of a role play garden area with less supervision. They may also be more appropriate for children under three who have not yet developed the coordination to use metal tools correctly.

■ There are a number a common 'mistakes' which can occur. When using a hand trowel to dig holes, ensure that they do not flick the soil up and into another child's eyes. Hand forks can have sharp points and therefore, when breaking up the soil, be careful that children are not sitting too closely together and may accidently injure another child. Full-sized forks and spades need careful coordination to use correctly and children may need supervision until they master this technique. Once again, watch they do not position the end above a stray hand or foot.

■ Tools should not be left lying on the ground where they can be stepped on or tripped over and be careful that hose pipes are not left unattended across paths.

■ Keep secateurs away from small hands – they may see you using them and want to have a go. Consider attaching them to elastic which can be tied onto your belt or wear a gardening apron with a large pocket.

Allergies

Although most children can spend time outside in the garden with few ill-effects, the high incidence of asthma and hayfever means that you may wish to avoid certain plants which can trigger an allergic reaction. The category of plants which most commonly cause problems are those which pollinate using the wind such as grasses, many native trees and some wild flowers. Pollen produced by these plants is carried by the wind and is easily inhaled. A low allergen garden would be one which avoids flowers which are heavily scented such as hyacinths and wisteria.

Insect pollinated plants are preferable as the pollen is less likely to be inhaled which generally includes flowers with large petals. Common plants which minimise the reaction to allergens include Hostas, *Aquilegia* and *Alchemilla Mollis*. Lightly scented shrubs and blossom-producing trees should also cause fewer problems. However you will need to balance an awareness of possible allergies with the desire to provide a multisensory garden. In some cases, it might be preferable to avoid the garden on very windy days when the pollen is at its greatest.

Some people will develop a skin reaction after touching certain plants such as Leyland cypress and chrysanthemums so it is best to avoid planting these. If an itchy rash does occur on a child's skin after visiting the garden, wash well with water and try to identify what may have been responsible so that they can avoid it in the future. Do not plant euphorbia or rue since the sap of these plants can produce a burning sensation which may be followed by blistering of the skin.

Poisonous plants

It is lovely to be able to wander around the garden with a group of children, selecting and tasting what you have grown. Berries seem all the more juicy for be eaten straight from the plant and even the most reluctant child may be tempted to try a small amount of chives which they have gathered themselves. However it is vital to educate children not to try anything which is growing without permission from a responsible adult first. Most children will have developed an understanding of this by the time they are three but there will always be exceptions. Very young children often explore the world by putting things in their mouths so it is important to be aware of what plants may potentially be harmful. Some plants are mildly poisonous whereas others can be deadly so it is vital that you learn to identify what the hazards are.

If you are developing an existing garden, spend time identifying the plants so that you can remove any which carry a particular risk. New plants bought at the garden centre should carry labels warning you of any dangers. Berries are particularly attractive to young children so restrict these to only those known to be entirely safe. For example, the attractive red berries of the yew tree could potentially be fatal if just one seed is eaten.

Plants to avoid include:

- Monkswood
- Deadly Nightshade
- Lily-of-the-valley
- Spurge Laurel
- Foxglove
- Laburnum
- Lupin
- Yew
- Wisteria
- Elder
- Opium Poppy
- Rowan
- Snowberry

Fortunately, many of these would need to be eaten in significant quantities and frequently they are accompanied by an unpleasant taste. However it is safest to avoid any species know to carry risks and in the event of unexplained nausea or diarrhoea, seek professional medical advice immediately.

Weather

The weather plays an important part in any garden. It contributes to healthy growth through rain and sun but can equally be responsible for the loss of plants through frost or drought. It similarly has a significant effect on the gardener. Some like nothing more than pottering around the garden on a scorching hot day whereas others prefer to visit on a damp morning and are fascinated by the effect of the dew on plants and cobwebs. A few simple steps will ensure that children can stay safe and comfortable in the garden all year round, whatever the weather.

Clothing

Ensure that the children have appropriate clothing by either insisting that bring in a set, or by supplying them yourselves. Wellies will keep feet dry although they do not always have non-slip soles. Hats are vital in strong sun and should ideally have both a peak and a flap to protect the neck.

Sun protection

During the summer months ensure you protect the children's skin through the use of sunscreen or, if not possible, encourage them to apply it at home in the morning.

Water

Children can soon become dehydrated if out in hot weather for a long period of time, particularly if they are involved in physical hard work. Ensure that there is an available source of fresh water and that children are encouraged to have regular drinks.

Shade

Incorporate a shaded area into the garden through careful planting of trees and shrubs. You will need to map the orientation of the sun as it changes throughout the day to identify where shade can be created without impacting upon the growth of plants. Alternatively, purchase a canopy which can be attached to a wall or upright posts. Fabric gazebos are now readily obtainable and are a relatively cheap way to create temporary shade wherever it is needed.

Involving everyone

A well organized garden will try to meet the needs all children, taking into account their various ages, abilities and backgrounds. Catering for everyone will make your garden rich and diverse; it will provide a range of experiences and inspire all to get involved.

Babies and very young children

You may need to give special consideration to the needs of children under the age of three. Small babies will enjoy the stimulation provided by a multisensory outdoor area and as they

grow, they will want to start exploring the varied environment. There are some simple steps that you can take to ensure that babies and very young children have access to natural physical and sensory experiences in the garden. Easy access to the garden is particularly important as some of the children will not be walking or will have limited mobility. Include an area in which you can support children with getting dressed in preparation for going outside. As they grow, they will become more independent and will take on greater responsibilities, such as in putting on Wellington boots or fetching tools. Where children cannot easily reach the garden to explore what is there, bring plants and produce to them. They will delight in investigating a sunflower head, giant pumpkin or simply a basket of leaves

Babies and toddlers are especially aware of different surfaces as much of their time will be spent lying, sitting or crawling on the ground. A variety of materials, such as grass, gravel, bark and timber decking can be used to stimulate and facilitate different learning experiences. Keep an area of soil for very young children to play in, practising the skills of digging and watering.

Create small slopes or steps to safely challenge children at different stages in their development, for example a grassy bank will test a baby who is learning to stand and will pose new challenges to a toddler trying to walk or roll down it.

Health and safety should be a priority when babies and very young children are out in the garden. Risk assessments should be carried out on a regular basis to ensure that the garden poses no unnecessary dangers. You should aim to reduce risks while also providing the children with opportunities and experiences that will allow them to develop skills and confidence.

Babies investigate new materials by putting them into their mouths so particular care must be taken when supervising their play, for example small stones could be a choking hazard. Appropriate shade and shelter should be provided so that babies and toddlers are not exposed to harmful or extreme weather conditions. Create a shaded area from fabric attached to trees or posts, or purchase a ready-made sunshade or gazebo. Balance the provision of shade with opportunities for children to experience different types of weather, such as feeling rain on their faces or snow on their hands.

Consider the effects created by light in different areas of the garden. Dappled shade will add interest for small babies. Light moves and creates changing shapes and shadows throughout the day and this will also fascinate the children. Grass may become prickly when exposed to full sunlight, whereas soft mosses may grow in shaded areas. Finally, ensure that you watch babies and very young children carefully if they have access to newly-seeded or planted areas of the garden. It is unfair to older children if their hard work in the garden is destroyed by the unintentional damage caused by the younger ones.

Special needs

Gardening provides the opportunity for children of all abilities to shine in different ways. When developing the outdoor garden, it is important to consider how you will meet the needs of all the children in your care. Catering for children with special needs will create a fully inclusive outdoor space. Consult with organizations, such as Mencap and the Gardening for Disabled Trust for specialist advice. You may also want to consider some of the points below.

Including surfaces that are suitable for those in wheelchairs or those who need assistance with walking. These surfaces should be hard, flat and even. Main pathways should be at least 1.5m wide with a gradient of no more than 1 in 15. You might need to install handrails to offer support with mobility.

Children who have special needs can become easily and frequently frustrated. Consider including an area for quiet reflection.

A common provision for children with special needs is a sensory garden. This is an area that focuses on heightening awareness of the surroundings through the senses. A sensory area will be beneficial to all children but especially to those who have sensory impairments or are on the autistic spectrum. You could theme your sensory garden to reflect a particular feature of the school or community or create a specific atmosphere. Use your imagination to stimulate the senses in different ways; are some suggestions for developing the senses.

Taste

Include common plants that can be safely picked and eaten, such as berries and herbs. Use easily-recognizable symbols to label plants that are safe to taste and ensure that there is nothing in the garden that could be harmful if eaten.

Sight

Think about adding variety in terms of colour, shape, size and contrast. Attempt to recreate a rainbow with colourful bedding plants or 'cool' and 'warm' plant containers. Try growing swiss chard ('Bright Lights'), an unusual vegetable with fantastic brightly-coloured stems and foliage. Incorporate interesting art features and add movement using water, flags or mobiles. Remember to use defined colours to add contrast to the edges

of paths or seats; this also makes it easier for children with visual impairments to navigate around the garden.

Smell

Include plants that release a range of different and unusual smells, rather than the more obvious floral scents, such as the curry plant or the chocolate-scented cosmos.

Some aromatic plants can be smelled from a distance whereas others can only be smelled when crushed by fingers or underfoot. Place aromatic plants near garden seating or between paving slabs so that the scents are released as people use the garden.

Touch

Point out and include a variety of textures for the children to touch. Leaves come in many different textures that range from rough to smooth. For example, Lamb's Ears (*Stachys Byzantina*), have a silky soft surface whereas Sedums have rubbery leaves. Position prickly plants out of reach so they do not cause harm.

Use different materials within the garden to create textural contrasts, such as smooth stone next to rough wood, or a cobble path leading to an area of soft long grass.

Sound

Nature produces its own interesting sounds that can be heard if you stop long enough to listen. Add sounds to the garden by planting Greater Quaking Grass (which will rustle in the wind) or

Case Study

In 2006, Fair Oak Infant School worked in partnership with Hampshire County Council to create the Children's World Garden supporting their strong focus on internationalism. Following an extensive consultation period in which the children were involved, the garden was created to include four zones: Australasia (which included grasslands), The Americas (which included a wigwam), Asia (which included a large Japanese archway) and Europe (which is included fruit trees). The garden had 12 flags linked to the 12 classes in the school; each class was named after a different country. The garden also included a maze, sheltered area and raised planting box. A lunchtime gardening club helped to maintain the garden with the support of a governor and parent. It provided an inspiring place to play during break times as well as a valuable learning resource.

Fair Oak Infant School, Hampshire

Home links

Organize a day to celebrate foods from around the world. Invite families to share the traditional dishes from their cultures and where possible use what you have grown in the garden to create a variety of foods for the children to try.

A multicultural garden can be an effective way to help develop relationships with families that you have problems communicating with due to language barriers. You can learn as much from them about their culture and also support them in developing a better understanding of the English language.

You may, for example, choose to develop an Asian garden. Plant an array of vegetables often used in Asian dishes such as ginger, green beans, eggplant, garlic, shallots, lemon grass, and a variety of leafy greens, basils and mints. Investigate cultural festivals and celebrations and link these to planting or harvesting. Explore the design elements commonly found in different gardens from around the world. For example, Japanese gardens often use symmetry and symbolism whereas Italian gardens favour upright supports such as trellises to maximise space.

bamboo (which creates a hollow noise when the stems knock together). Wind-chimes, running water, and fixed outdoor musical instruments can all add to the interesting sounds of the garden.

Making links with parents and the local community

An early years garden can bring parents and the local community together, building valuable and lasting relationships. By involving parents and carers in the development of your garden, they are given the chance to play a greater role in their children's development outside of the home. Their involvement will help them to develop a better understanding of their children's educational experiences and in turn supports staff by giving them an insight into the family life of the children in their care.

Parents and other family members can be involved throughout the project in many different ways, such as fundraising, planning, researching, publicising, and helping to create the garden. Keep them well informed about garden developments and be sure to value their contributions, however small. Host a 'work party' day to bring everyone together in a productive and enjoyable way. You can also use the photocopiable sheets on the following two pages to give to parents so that they can support their child's new-found gardening skills at home.

Grandparents can be very knowledgeable about gardening and you might look at ways to get them involved. They may have more free time than parents to offer regular support in caring for the garden and sharing their skills. Cross-generational links are a valuable way of benefitting all age groups. Gardening is something that is as appealing to men as women and may provide an excellent way to introduce the children in your setting to positive male and female role models.

Some of the ways in which you might develop valuable links with your local community include:

■ Donations from local garden centres and nurseries.

■ Expertise from members of a gardening club or local allotment society.

■ Partnership with a local secondary school. Involve them in creating an art feature for the garden.

■ Working with people who have specialist skills, such as a bricklayer, carpenter or landscape architect. They might consider offering their services at a reduced rate in return for positive publicity.

■ Contacting your local theatre to see if performers might support the official opening of the garden.

■ Seeking out businesses to carry out team-building days for their staff by assisting with building or painting tasks.

■ Looking for ways to link to local events, such as entering a village or town show, creating a garden-themed carnival float or by hiring a market stall for a week.

■ Contacting the local press. They are usually enthusiastic about including pictures of children with a giant sunflower or enormous pumpkin so invite them to come and photograph your children's successes.

Multicultural enrichment

A 'multicultural garden' is one that celebrates cultural diversity and can develop stronger links throughout the local community. Look at growing fruit, vegetables and herbs from across the world and use these to share information about their uses in different cultures. Where possible involve children from different cultural backgrounds and their families in choosing what to grow. They may be more familiar with their native plants and what it is possible to grow in a British climate. If you are lucky they might already be growing such plants in their own gardens and could provide donations of seeds or plants. Alternatively, you may need to use specialist nurseries for some of the more exotic plants you wish to grow.

Garden activities to try at home

We aim to help your child to develop a greater understanding and love of the natural world through the use of our garden. You can support this in many ways at home and we would like to hear about your greatest discoveries and achievements! Here are some ideas to get you started.

If you have never grown your own food before, create a mini edible garden at home. Vegetables often need very little space – containers can be made from many unusual recycled objects such as an old tyre or broken wheelbarrow. Just ensure they have sufficient drainage and fill with compost. Plants can be grown from seed or bought cheaply as small plants at your local market. You may find that your child is more enthusiastic about home-grown vegetables than those from the supermarket!

If you have a chance please come and visit our garden and talk to your child about what they have done there. And please do not mind if they come home looking a little grubby around the edges – it probably means they have had a fantastic time outdoors!

Spend time with your child visiting a local greengrocers, farmers' market or farm shop. Have a look at what is on sale and think about where the produce was grown. Choosing local foods ensures that we are eating fruit and vegetables when they are most fresh and in season. It also cuts down on harmful pollution caused by the needless transportation of foods around the world.

With such busy lives nowadays, it can sometimes be difficult to commit to caring for a garden. Often, it is the older generation who have the necessary time and skills to inspire today's children to become involved in gardening. Do you know anyone, maybe a grandparent or elderly neighbour who would love the opportunity to show your child how to grow and care for plants?

Encourage your child to notice the changing seasons where they live. What grows around your home at different times of year, what types of weather do they see? Perhaps you could make scrapbook, updating it each month as your surroundings change. You could include photos, pressed flowers and leaves or pictures of any wildlife you have seen. This would make a lovely record of their home to keep for when they are older.

How about buying your child a range of garden tools suitable for small hands for their next birthday? Garden centres and supermarkets often sell well made and reasonably priced tools which are likely to inspire your child to go outside and start growing!

Create a nature table at home. Each time your child collects a natural 'treasure' on a walk or at the park, display it for a while and perhaps try to discover more about it.

Using what we grow

The value of your garden goes well beyond sowing the seeds and caring for the plants as they grow. Hopefully you will be rewarded with a varied harvest which can then be used in many exciting ways.

Cooking and Eating

One of the most valuable benefits of developing a garden is to give children a greater understanding of how food is grown. They love the opportunity to cook with crops harvested straight from their garden and through this, can be encouraged to try foods which they might otherwise avoid. Linking what you have grown to tasty, attractive dishes which the children can help to prepare, supports government healthy eating schemes such as the Five A Day campaign and Jamie Oliver's Feed Me Better project.

There are many organisations and websites out there who are promoting the chance for young children to get hands-on experience of the cycle of seed to plate. Dorset Cereals have an excellent website www.edibleplaygrounds.co.uk which is campaigning to make it government policy that every child has access to food growing in their playground so that they can develop a better understanding of where food comes from. The Grow Your Own Grub website from Growing Schools (www.growinggrub.co.uk) has a wealth of information on running an outdoor food-growing project and ways to link this to healthy cooking and eating.

Some of your produce, such as berries and tomatoes, can be picked and eaten straight from the plant when it is at its most fresh and juicy. Other fruits and vegetables will need to be cooked and this is a fantastic opportunity to involve the children in preparing simple and delicious meals. You may wish to involve the local community in sharing the feast by inviting them in for a delicious buffet meal.

Produce can be used to create both sweet and savoury dishes. You may wish to challenge children's preconceptions by using unexpected fruits or vegetables in their cooking such as carrots in a cake or strawberries in a savoury salad. Where possible involve the children in the whole cooking process from washing and chopping the vegetables to plating up and sharing the finished dishes. In some dishes, such as baked apples or vegetable pizzas, the main fruit or vegetable will still be easy

Home links

If you have a bountiful harvest, consider sending surplus produce home with the children. Perhaps you could include an appropriate recipe which the children can follow with their families, see the next two pages for inspiration.

to recognise. However, you could choose recipes which allow the children to challenge others to identify the ingredients such as a sweet pumpkin pie or rhubarb crumble. Do not forget to include herbs to flavour the dishes and seeds such as sunflowers or pumpkin. Edible flowers make a surprising treat- try sweet-tasting *Nasturtium* flowers in a salad or rose petal ice cream.

Below are some tasty recipes for you to try:

Apple muffins (serves 12)

Ingredients

255g (9 oz) plain flour
110g (4 oz) apples - peeled, cored and chopped
100g (4 oz) caster sugar
225ml (8 fl oz) semi-skimmed milk
60g (2 oz) butter
3 teaspoons baking powder
1/2 teaspoon salt

- Preheat oven to 200°C/Gas Mark 6. Line a 12-cup muffin tin with paper muffin cups.

- In a large bowl, sift together the flour, baking powder and salt.

- In a separate bowl, cream together the sugar and butter. Stir the flour mixture into the sugar mixture alternately with the milk. Fold in the fruit. Pour the batter into the prepared muffin tin.

- Bake in a preheated oven for 20 to 25 minutes.

Vegetable pizza (serves 8)

Ingredients

Large readymade pizza base or pizza dough prepared in a breadmaker for ease
200g mozzarella cheese – cubed
180g (6oz) plum tomatoes – chopped
1 tablespoon olive oil
1/2 medium onion – finely chopped
Assorted toppings depending upon what you have grown – peppers, mushrooms, sweetcorn, spinach, courgettes, basil, oregano – chopped

- Prepare the dough if making from scratch. The children will love kneading and shaping it into mini pizzas.

- In a small saucepan heat up the oil to medium-high, add the onion and saute for 5-6 minutes. Add the tomatoes and turn down to medium-low heat and simmer for 10-15 minutes.

- Spread the tomato sauce over the bases and evenly distribute the rest of the toppings. Sprinkle with cheese.

- Place the pizzas on a preheated baking tray or pizza stone and cook for 8-10 minutes.

Case Study

Little Dragons is a small Forest School nursery set within the grounds of a village primary school. It shares the school gardens for composting and growing vegetables as well as having its own small garden which contains endless pots and containers of flowers and herbs. Since nobody on the team is a natural gardener, they asked for help by newsletter and with the help of a few parents and lots of muddy enthusiasm, they have developed a 'quaintly untidy but healthy and energetic garden.' The children like nothing more than planting, tending, picking and cooking their own food. They love to experiment with new tastes and textures because they have grown the food themselves and the parents are constantly amazed and pleased at what the children will eat. The nursery is almost entirely organic, sourcing much of its produce from the local butcher, farmer and allotment owners.

Little Dragons Nursery, Northants

Strawberry mousse (serves 6)

Ingredients

225g strawberries (halved) and 25g for decoration
150g mini marshmallows
25g caster sugar
200ml double cream
100ml water

- Gently cook the strawberries in the water over a low heat until they are soft enough to mash.

- Remove from the heat and squash the strawberries with a fork.

- Add the marshmallow, mixing them well until they melt. Allow to cool.

- Whip the cream and then fold into the strawberry mixture.

- Spoon into small pots and place in the fridge to chill.

- Decorate with remaining strawberries

You could use raspberries instead of strawberries if you have these in your garden.

Veggie kebabs

Ingredients

A selection of fresh vegetables such as tomatoes, peppers, courgettes, aubergine, mushrooms

1 tbsp vinegar
3 tbsp olive oil

- Cut the vegetables into chunks and thread onto skewers.

- Mix the oil and vinegar together and brush onto the vegetables.

- Cook on a barbeque or under the grill for 10-15 minutes, turning regularly.

- Either cut off the pointed end of the skewer before giving to young children, or use a fork to slide the vegetables onto a plate.

Carrot cake

Ingredients

150g grated carrots
100g any dried fruit such as raisins or glace cherries
100g self raising flour
100g soft brown sugar
5 tbsp sunflower oil
2 medium eggs

- Preheat the oven to 190°C/ Gas Mark 5.

- Mix together the eggs and sugar.

- Beat in the oil.

- Mix in the carrot, flour and dried fruit.

- Spoon into muffin cases and cook for 15-20 minutes until golden brown.

Selling and Sharing

Sale of produce

Once you have your growing garden up and running, it should not be long until you have a surplus of produce which you need to find a good home for. You may also shut during the summer and wish to avoid the complications of finding someone to continue to water containers or baskets. Consider having a summer sale to sell off crops and flowers, raising useful funds to support the following season's activities. This may be as large or small as you wish but will enable the children to take pride in what they have produced and share it with the local community.

Involve the children in promoting the sale, by making posters or designing a flyer to take home. Flowers can be tied in handy bunches with raffia and kept fresh in a bucket of water. You may be happy to sell off containers, particularly if the children have decorated them themselves. Request that baskets are returned in the autumn so they can be refilled the following year. If you are short on produce, ask for donations from parents of homemade preserves or cakes to add to the stall. Price goods up clearly and encourage the children to collect and later count the money.

Alternatively, you might like to give away unwanted produce. It is likely to be welcomed by a local retirement home, particularly if the children are able to personally deliver it and share with the older generation their successes and failures. You may have a local shelter for the homeless that would value the gift of fresh fruit and vegetables, helping to educate the children about caring for those who are less fortunate.

Celebrations

Gardens and their produce provide a wonderful starting point for a celebration. Many religions throughout the world celebrate outdoors or give thanks for the harvest and by marking these occasions you can help to bring the local community together. You might also consider organising a non-religious celebration in your outdoor area which can be linked to a seasonal event or particular success. Some possible ideas include:

- **Easter:** Decorate your garden in preparation for a special Easter egg hunt. Easter usually falls just as the garden is beginning to wake up after the winter and is an excellent time to encourage the children to go outside and look for the first signs of spring. Foil wrapped chocolate eggs can be hidden through the undergrowth for the children to discover. Ensure that you warn them to take particular care around newly emerging bulbs and new shoots. Ask them to imagine that they have eyes in their toes!

- **Baisakhi:** This is one of the major Sikh festivals and is celebrated enthusiastically in the Punjab and around the world. Falling in the middle of April, it marks the time when they harvest the crops and it is celebrated the day before with music and dance. Weather-permitting, consider venturing out into the garden for the first picnic of the year

- **Well Dressing:** Well dressing is an ancient tradition which originated In the Peak District. It is now practised in many rural communities in which wells or other sources of water are decorated in flower petals to make attractive designs.

- **Harvest:** Thanksgiving celebrations for a successful harvest take place worldwide in many different cultures. In Britain, we have celebrated the bringing in of the crops since pagan times usually by singing, praying and decorating our churches with baskets of fruit and vegetables. This usually takes place during September or October.

- **Tree Dressing Day:** Tree dressing is based on many old customs from all over the world and at different times of the year. It encourages the celebration of trees and helps to remind us of their importance to us all. In this country, it is organised by Common Ground and takes place in the first week of December. You might wish to select a single tree to be dressed each year, or create a magical forest by decorating many trees. Use shiny, reflective materials which catch the light, encouraging the children to design their own decorations.

- **Halloween:** The celebration of All Hallows Eve has grown greatly in this country over the past few years. If you choose to organise your own Halloween event, create the feeling of magic and mystery with carved pumpkins or squashes, silhouettes of bats cut from black plastic bags, a cauldron full of mystical potion using plants gathered from the garden and a bowl of water with apples to bob.

- **Apple Day:** This celebration of local varieties of apples takes place on 21st October each year and is a fantastic time to explore your own harvest of apples. Try out new apple recipes or plant a few local apple trees.

Activities linked to the garden

The garden is one of the most useful resources that you can develop within your setting. It can provide you with endless opportunities to develop enjoyable, simple activities, which meet one or more of the Early Learning Goals set out in the Early Years Foundation Stage. Your setting's garden should regularly provide inspiration for new ideas because it is always changing; from season to season and from year to year. It will give children opportunities to explore the natural world and develop their own interests.

Knowledge and Understanding of the World

Investigate objects and materials by using all their senses

- Ask the children to collect tiny pieces of leaves or flower petals and mix them with a small amount of water to create a 'smelly cocktail'. Show them how to crush the plant material between their fingers to release the smell. Ask: 'What happens to the water when the plants are added?' They might also like to come up with a suitable name for their cocktail. Use this as an opportunity to discuss the importance of not putting anything in their mouths without adult supervision.

- If you are growing herbs in your garden, ask the children to collect some of those with the most attractive scent. Cut the ends from pairs of tights and fill with a selection of the fragrant herbs. These can be tied with pretty ribbon and, when hung below the hot tap on a bath, will produce relaxing, perfumed water

Build and construct with a wide range of objects

- Give the children a wide range of natural resources and encourage them to think about which ones they would use to create a wildlife hotel. Pallets can be used if stacked on top of one another to create the structure with bundles of

bamboo, bricks, soil, moss and cardboard pushed into each layer to create the "rooms" for minibeasts, frogs and maybe even a hedgehog.

- Challenge the children to create traps to prevent pests from damaging their crops. What pests do they need to capture? How will the collect the pests without them escaping? What will they use to lure the pests into the traps? Solutions might include jam jars with a small amount of milk at the bottom, hollowed out oranges or sticky paper. Ensure that you are not also trapping wildlife such as ladybirds or bees which may be beneficial to your garden.

Select the tools and techniques they need to shape, assemble and join the materials they are using

- Help the children to create a watering system that will keep their plants watered when there is no-one else available to do it. Provide them with a range of resources, such as buckets or watering cans with holes in the bottom, guttering, tubing and plastic bottles. Can they work out how to transport the water or regulate its flow?

Observe, find out about and identify features in the place they live and the natural world

■ Cover the bottom of the tray with a layer of compost and then use a range of natural and scrap materials to represent different features of the garden. Suggest that the children represent themselves in the garden using small world figures showing what they like doing the most.

■ Encourage the children to come up with a way to record and share everything they are doing in the setting's garden. They might want to keep a journal with lots of drawings and photos. They could create a display board for parents or contribute to a regular newsletter for families. Let the children decide what information they think is most important to share; they might be more excited about a pile of slugs in a homemade trap than their bumper crop of tomatoes!

■ Create a 'vegetable-top world' together. The ends of many vegetables, often thrown away in the preparation of food, can be used to create a growing jungle. Place the vegetables tops (such as parsnips, carrots and turnips) in a shallow saucer of water. Soon the leaves will start to sprout creating a magical world for the children to observe.

■ Place a map, displayed on the wall, to encourage the children to think about how far their food has travelled. Invite them to collect stickers from their fruit snacks or labels from vegetables brought in from home and stick them onto the relevant countries. Ask them to start to thinking about their own produce in the setting's garden and how this has a less harmful impact upon the environment.

Identify some features of objects

■ Bury a range of natural and man-made objects in your compost heap, for example an apple or flower, or a plastic brick and toy car. Ask the children: 'Which ones do you think will break down to form compost?' Have a look a few weeks later as your aerate your heap to see which objects remain a nd which have disappeared. Where do the children think the natural objects have gone?

Begin to know about their own cultures and beliefs

■ Try to grow crops that reflect the ethnic backgrounds of the children in your setting. Parents or grandparents may be able to advise and might even be willing to supply

seeds or seedlings. Some plants will be unsuitable to our climate or may need to be kept indoors, such as ginger, which can be successfully grown from a small piece of ginger root.

Observe and find out about the natural world

■ Place a garden snail on a piece of clear Perspex and watch it from underneath to see how it moves along. Put some flour paste near to the snail and tell the children to watch it eating using its mouth (the *radula*) Try this with other animals, such as worms and beetles, and ask the children to observe how they move differently to the snail.

■ Experiment making a 'cress head'. Fill the end of an old pair of tights with some compost mixed with cress seeds; form the cut off end into a nose, securing it with an elastic band. Use sticky shapes or pens to decorate the heads leaving the hair area untouched. Place each head in a saucer of water, refilling when necessary. Gradually the cress will start to grow and it will look like hair. When the hair gets very long, supervise the children to give their 'cress heads' a hair cut; the cress can also be a tasty snack. Alternatively, try growing cress in an egg shell or in a coconut with the top removed.

■ Pick a selection of flowers on a warm, dry day choosing those plants without woody stems such as pansies, daisies and geraniums. Carefully arrange between sheets of blotting paper and either place in a flower press or use a number of heavy

books to weigh them down. After three to four weeks they can be removed and used to create cards or pictures.

- Hyacinth bulbs have traditionally been placed in special hourglass containers filled with water to view both the roots and the flowers as they grow. A cheaper alternative is to use jam jars. Allow each child to create their own name label and tie it around a jar with a ribbon. Fill each jar with water so that the bulb sits just above but is not touching the water. Place the jars in a cool dark place, such as a shed, until a good root system has formed. This may take eight to ten weeks. Bring the bulbs out into a warm, light position and keep the water levels topped up to allow the shoots to start to grow. Beware of letting children handle hyacinth bulbs as they can irritate the skin.

Physical Development

Move with confidence, imagination and in safety

- Encourage the children to study how different minbeasts from their garden move around. Can they recreate these movements themselves? Give them props to support this, such as chiffon scarves to represent the wings of a butterfly, toilet rolls which can be slowly unwound as they crawl along the floor to represent a slug's slime trail or sheets to wriggle under as they become an earthworm tunnelling to safety.

Find appropriate music to play as they move, such as the *Flight of the Bumble Bee* by Nikolai Rimsky-Korsakov.

Use a range of small and large equipment

- Collect different coloured and shaped petals and blossom and place these on a tray. How many petals can the children pick up and place in a cup (by sucking them onto the end of a straw) in one minute? Vary the game by asking them to collect petals or blossom of a single colour.

Handle tools, objects, construction and malleable materials safely and with increasing control

- Teach the children how to use gardening tools appropriately. Some children will have parents or grandparents who use gardening tools at home and so will be familiar with them. For others, it will be a new experience, so do not assume that they know the correct way to use a hand fork or garden rake. Involve them in looking after the tools, including cleaning them at the end of a session and storing them away safely.

Travel around, under, over and through

- Design a treasure hunt in and around the garden by hiding items such as chocolate mini eggs or large pieces of a jigsaw.

Establish clear rules for the hunt, such as where the children can go without harming the plants. Hide some of the items low down so that they have to crawl under bushes and some high up so that they have to stretch to retrieve them from trees.

- Go for a walk in the rain together. Ensure that the children have suitable clothing and then take a small group out into the garden. See how far they can get without getting wet by Encouraging the children to look for good places to shelter. They will soon discover that a thick canopy of leaves from a mature tree is more effective than a bush, which will quickly soak them if they try to hide within its branches. Are there any large leaves, such as those from a rhubarb plant, which can be used as makeshift umbrellas? Observe which animals, such as worms and snails, have come out to enjoy the rain.

Recognise the importance of keeping healthy and those things which contribute to this

- Read *Oliver's Vegetables* by Vivian French and encourage the children to try a new vegetable, which they have grown themselves, each day for a week.

- Use produce from your setting's garden to cook with. Involve the children in harvesting and preparing the dishes so that they are more enthusiastic to try them!

Creative Development

Explore colour, texture, shape, form and space in two and three dimension

- Give each child a ball of play dough. Instruct them to form the dough into magical creatures called hobgoblins and find homes for them within the garden. Use natural materials to develop the characters, such as an upturned flower for a hat or sticks for arms. Alternatively, use the play dough to form tree faces by pressing the dough onto the bark to create unusual faces with knobbly noses and warty skin.

- If you have grown pumpkins, ask the children to design faces that can then be drawn onto them. Involve the children in scooping out the flesh and then carefully cut around the designs before gently pushing the pieces out. Use the flesh to make pumpkin pie.

- Collect seed cases, tree parts and other natural items from around your garden. Provide the children with

photographs of minibeasts to inspire them to design their own bugs using the natural materials and other craft items, such as pipe cleaners and wobbly stick-on eyes.

- Allow the children to build their own bird nests. Look at pictures of different types of nests; all varieties of birds build their nests in slightly different ways using a range of materials. Collect suitable nesting resources, such as twigs, leaves, moss, lichen, feathers, grass and sheep's wool. As the children are forming their nests, remind them that the purpose of a nest is to support and insulate the eggs and baby birds. Explain that adult birds have to make hundreds of journeys to collect the materials for their nests because each piece is gathered individually.

Independent and guided exploration of and engagement with a widening range of media and materials

- Use natural materials to create pictures and patterns in the style of Andy Goldsworthy or Giuseppe Archimboldo. These could be arranged on card and photographed for a lasting record. If you have a cold spell during the winter, allow the children to create designs from natural materials in shallow containers of water and then place them outside overnight to freeze. A less chilly method is to preserve them in dishes of concentrated clear gelatine. These nature jellies will only last for a few days but have an underwater quality when they have set.

- Leaves provide many opportunities to explore different media. Ask the children to collect the most colourful leaves they can find to make a collage. Encourage them to take rubbings from the backs of the leaves to explore the different shapes and textures, or laminate the leaves to create an autumn-inspired window decoration.

Natural materials can be use to produce interesting marks when pressed into play dough or clay. Collect a range of resources, such as sweet chestnut cases, pine cones, conkers and crab apples. Can other children guess which natural items made the play dough or clay impressions?

Sing simple songs from memory.

There are many traditional nursery rhymes that include references to flowers, such as *Ring a Ring O'Roses*, *Lavender Blue* and *Mary, Mary Quite Contrary*. Many of these have rather unpleasant connections to historical events, which are likely to be unsuitable for discussion with young children. However, they might like to find the plants referred to within their own garden.

Recognise repeated sounds and sounds patterns.

It is possible to grow gourds and ornamental squashes which can then be dried and used as instruments. The seeds inside make an attractive sound when shaken and in Africa gourds were traditionally used for scaring birds.

Explore colour

Ask the children to colour in paper cutouts of moths so that they are camouflaged in the garden. Half of the group can they hide their moths outside and the remainder of the children must try to find them. How well camouflaged were they?

Make a beautiful display together by dyeing squares of cotton fabric with natural dyes. Strawberries, raspberries, blackberries and spinach can all be crushed and added to a little water to produce effective cold-water dyes. Other vegetables will need to be boiled to release the dyes, such as beetroot, carrots, red cabbage and onion skins. Help the children to assemble the squares of fabric to make a natural rainbow quilt.

Create paper bracelets for the children with stripes of different colours. Fix double-sided clear tape around the bracelets and peel off the backing paper once they are in place. The children must try to match small pieces of natural materials to the colours on their bracelets and attach them to the tape. Sample colour cards from a DIY store can also be used to encourage older children to look for different shades of the same colour.

Developing imagination and imaginative play

■ Create a garden that represents the elements of a story. You might want to choose a fairytale, such as Jack and The Beanstalk or something more contemporary such as *The Very Hungry Caterpillar*. Use the flowers as a paint palette to create pictures (in the style of traditional municipal parks) and add the children's artwork, such as clay figures or features made from junk materials, to retell the story. The children can add to and develop this over time, perhaps adding their own elements to the scene.

■ Set up garden-themed imaginative play areas, such as a garden centre or farmers' market and encourage the children to choose what they want to sell. Use real produce or make it from junk materials, tissue paper, clay or simply pictures cut out from catalogues and laminated.

Personal, Social and Emotional Development

Being interested, excited and motivated to learn

■ Help the children to grow potatoes within a stack of old car tyres. First of all, place the seed potatoes on a windowsill for a few weeks to allow them to sprout (known as chitting'), then cover them with soil with the shoots facing upwards. As the shoots reappear, cover them with more soil (this is known as earthing up) and add an additional tyre as needed. Keep the shoots well-watered and feed them every couple of weeks. The potatoes will be ready to be discovered in the early summer.

Have a developing awareness of their own needs, views and feelings

■ Create a sensory area within the garden using plants to stimulate the senses, such as rustling grass to hear; Lambs' Ears (*Stachys Byzantine*) to touch; herbs to smell and taste; brightly-coloured annuals to see. Discuss how the plants make the children feel. When might they choose to go to the sensory area?

■ Explain to the children the ways in which people used to communicate their feelings by using flowers. For example,

people who were too shy to express their emotions would give others small posies called 'tussie mussies', which had hidden meanings. Honeysuckle represented devotion and roses were used to express love. Talk about how flowers are used to express emotions in the present day.

Understand what is right, what is wrong and why

■ Support the children in developing a number of rules for the garden. This may include respecting plants and wildlife as well as safety issues. You might wish to have a permanent sign made, particularly if there are other visitors to the garden.

Be sensitive to the needs, views and feelings of others

■ Identify a tree in your grounds that can be used to display thoughts or feelings. The children's ideas can be written or drawn onto paper leaves, which can then be laminated and hung from the branches. You might want to allocate a 'feelings tree' for expressing different emotions, or a 'peace tree' to explore the ways in which they can learn to get along with others.

■ Show the children how to care for the wildlife in the garden, especially in the winter. Provide extra food for birds by mixing lard, breadcrumbs and seeds and then pressing the mixture into a bird feeder or an old nylon onion bag. Never put whole peanuts out in the spring or summer as these can cause baby birds to choke.

Form good relationships with adults

■ Gifts that link to the garden can be used to celebrate special occasions, such as Mothers' or Fathers' Day. An unusual gift to create is a 'cress' mum or dad. Place several layers of paper

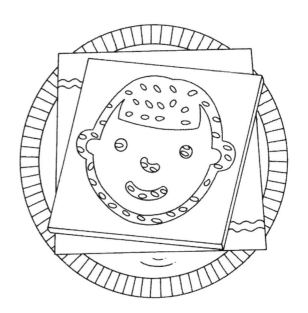

towels on a paper plate and dampen the tissue slightly with water. Cut out a stencil of a man or woman and place it over the damp tissue. Ask the children to sprinkle cress seeds over the tissue but not on the stencil. Once the stencil is removed, it will leave a shape of a figure. Keep the seeds moist and over the next few days the outline of a a 'cress' mum or dad will grow, which can then be carefully taken home.

Respond to significant experiences, showing a range of feelings when appropriate

■ Gardening provides perfect opportunities to explore life cycles and how different stages of development make children feel. The long awaited first shoot from a bean might make them feel excited and proud, whereas a drought-induced plant death is an opportunity to explore disappointment. Exploring wildlife can also inspire discussions, such as the joy of discovering newly-hatched baby birds or frogspawn found in the pond.

Work as part of a group, taking turns and sharing fairly

■ Your setting's garden should be 'owned' jointly by everyone involved in its care. At all stages from sowing to harvesting, the children will soon discover the benefits of working together as a team. You may wish to give groups of children

special responsibilities or their own area to care for. This is a valuable way to encourage children to value the successes of others and to empathize with disappointments when things do not go as they had hoped.

Dress and undress independently and manage their own personal hygiene.

■ In order to use the garden, the children will have to learn how to care for themselves. There will be plenty of opportunities for them to learn how to dress appropriately for all types of gardening weather throughout the year. This will include putting on suitable clothing and footwear and also learning about hygiene, such as washing their hands after gardening.

Communication, Language and Literacy

Developing an understanding of the correspondence between spoken and written sounds

■ Use low growing annuals, such as Poached Egg Plants (*Limnanthes*) to spell out letters or words in the soil. Assist the children to mark out the letters with sand and then sprinkle the seeds finely over the top. Cover lightly with soil and wait for the 'magic writing' to emerge. Alternatively, spell out words on a larger scale by planting bulbs set into a grassy area. For instant writing, try spelling out words on a path using sugar; ants will soon be attracted to the sugar and watch them form living letters!

Respond to stories

■ Read a range of relevant stories to the children. There are several books that link to the theme of 'growing'. Try *Eddie's Garden and How to Make Things Grow* by Sarah Garland or *Jasper's Beanstalk* by Mick Inkpen.

Interact with others, negotiating plans and activities and taking turns in conversation

■ Encourage the children to work together when caring for the garden. There are so many things they will want to talk about from what plants they should grow to how to care for them.

■ Send the children a surprise letter containing a mystery bean. Ask them who they think sent it, what they think it might grow into and how they think they should look after it.

Retell a narrative in the correct sequence

■ Discuss with the children how you might make a scarecrow. Think about the individual steps needed and once you have built it, see if the children can recount the process in the correct order. Use the scarecrow as a stimulus for storytelling. Read children's books about scarecrows, such as *The Scarecrow* by Gina Thompson or *Tattybogle* by Sandra Ann Horn.

Attempt writing for different purposes.

■ Support the children in creating their own labels for what they are growing. Draw or write the names of the plants onto paper and then laminate them so that they are more hardwearing.

Extend their vocabulary, exploring the meanings and sounds of new words.

■ Place objects found within the garden in small fabric bags (old socks or thick tights will do). Invite the children to put their hands inside the bags (without looking) and describe what they are touching. They will need to use a wide range of adjectives to tell others what the object feels like. This activity can be repeated using objects with a strong smell, for example ask them to describe what it smells like and whether it is something they like.

Problem Solving, Reasoning and Numeracy

Use numbers as labels and for counting

Sing songs that include counting, such as:

Five little flowers standing in the sun
(Hold up five fingers.)
See their heads nodding, bowing one by one?
(Bend fingers several times.)
Down, down, down comes the gentle rain.
(Raise hands, wiggle fingers and lower arms to simulate falling rain.)
And the five little flowers lift their heads up again!
(Hold up five fingers.)

And

Five spring flowers, all in a row.
The first one said, 'We need rain to grow!'
The second one said, 'Oh my, we need water!'
The third one said, 'Yes, it is getting hotter!'
The fourth one said, 'I see clouds in the sky.'
The fifth one said, 'I wonder why?'

Then BOOM went the thunder
And ZAP went the lightning!
That springtime storm was really frightening!
But the flowers weren't worried – no, no, no, no!
The rain helped them to grow, grow, grow!

Use language to describe mathematical concepts

■ There are so many ways in which children can explore their harvest. You might want to create a 'recording station' to do this. Give the children clipboards and old white shirts to wear so that they become the researchers. Provide them with the necessary tools, such as scales and rulers and encourage them to count, weigh and measure what they have grown.

■ Give each child a pretty, decorated envelope labelled 'Race to the Sun' containing several sunflower seeds. Challenge them to see who can grow the tallest sunflower by September. On the given date, invite the parents in for an official measuring party with refreshments and prizes for all.

■ Fill a sink or an old baby bath with water and challenge the children to predict which of the vegetables they have grown will sink or float. Will the largest ones sink or will it be those that are the heaviest? Turn the ones that float into boats with the aid of sticks and paper sails.

Count reliably up to ten

■ Use seeds harvested from sunflowers, or dried beans for counting games.

Use everyday words to describe position

■ Talk about where crops grow. Create a display that shows which fruit or vegetables grow under the ground, those that rest upon the soil and those that grow on climbers or in trees.

Talk about, recognise and recreate simple patterns

■ Use garden produce to create printed patterns on paper. Vegetables, such as apples and potatoes, can be dipped into paint to make the patterns. The children could also print patterns onto terracotta pots, using water-based paints mixed with PVA glue to make them waterproof.

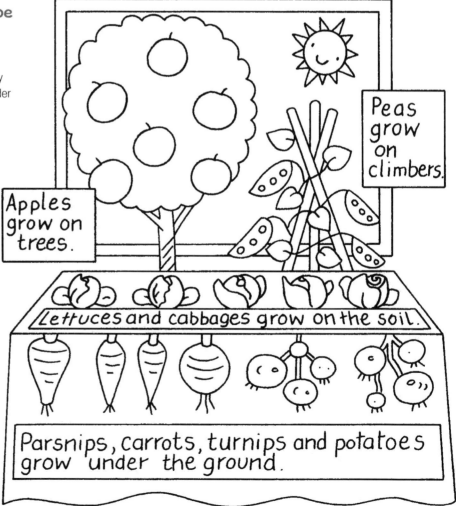

Further resources

Useful organizations

Royal Horticultural Society
RHS Wisley, Woking, Surrey, GU23 6QB
Web: www.rhs.org.uk/schoolgardening

The Royal Horticultural Society runs the 'Campaign for School Gardening' to support settings in the development and use of gardens within their grounds. It includes a benchmarking scheme to reward progression, and regular training opportunities countrywide. Membership is free.

Garden Organic
Ryton Organic Gardens, Coventry, CV8 3LG
Tel: 024 7630 8238
Email: enquiry@schoolsorganic.net
Web: www.schoolsorganic.net

Garden organic have a membership scheme called 'Garden Organic for Schools', which provides resources to help schools set up and manage organic vegetable gardens. You can register for free on their website.

Learning Through Landscapes
Third Floor, Southside Offices, The Law Courts, Winchester, SO23 9DL
Tel: 01962 846258
Web: www.ltl.org.uk

It is possible to join this organization for an annual fee. They cater for early years settings by providing bimonthly mailings; access to a wealth of resources on the website; funding information and discounted training opportunities.

National Federation of City Farms and Community Gardens
The Greenhouse, Hereford Street, Bedminster, Bristol, BS3 4NA
Tel: 0117 9231800
Web: www.farmgarden.org.uk

Growing Schools
Web: www.growingschools.org.uk

This is a Department of Children, Schools and Families programme that encourages schools to use the outdoors as an educational resource. The website has excellent resources for

teachers and early years practitioners to support them in using gardens and grounds.

The Royal Society of Prevention Of Accidents (RoSPA)
Web: www.rospa.com
Information available about safety in the garden.

Common Ground
Gold Hill House, 21 High Street, Shaftesbury, Dorset, SP7 8JE
Tel: 01747 850820
Web: www.commonground.org.uk

Further websites

www.bbc.co.uk/gardening/gardening_with_children/
Excellent website with ideas and resources about involving children in gardening.

www.edibleplaygrounds.co.uk
Resources to encourage children to grow and cook.

www.gardeningwithchildren.co.uk
Useful resources for schools.

www.littlerotters.org.uk
Practical information and advice on composting.

www.mindstretchers.co.uk
Wide range of equipment and books for use outdoors

www.thegrowingschoolsgarden.org.uk
Interactive site to encourage use of spaces beyond the classroom.

www.wigglywigglers.co.uk
Good site for mail-order wildlife gardening and composting with entertaining podcasts.

Books

Bradley C (1997) *The Family Garden*. Lorenz Books

Danks F, Schofield J (2005) *Natures Playground*. Frances Lincoln

Harries J (2008) *Planning for Learning Through Growth*. Practical Pre-School Books, London

Lockie B (2007) *Gardening with Young Children*. Hawthorn Press

Lovejoy S (1999) *Roots, Shoots, Buckets and Boots* (Gardening Together with Children). Workman Publishing

Matthews C (2002) *Great Gardens for Kids*. Hamlyn

Murphy D (2008) *The Playground Potting Shed*. Guardian Books

Rhoades D (1995) *Garden Crafts for Kids*. Sterling

RHS (2008) *Grow it Eat it*. Dorling Kindersley

Sayles Hughes M, Hughes T (2000) *Buried Treasure (Plants We Eat)*. Lerner Publishing Company

Sykes R (2006) *Edible Gardens in Schools*. Southgate

Walton S (2000) *I Can Grow Things: How-to-Grow Activity Projects for the Very Young (Show-me-how)*. Lorenz Books

Wilde K (2005) *Gardening with Children*. Collins

Woram C, Cox M (2008) *Gardening with Kids*. Ryland Peters and Small

Glossary of terms

Annual
A plant grown from seed which only lives for one year

Bare root plants
Usually trees, hedges or roses which are dug up and sold while they are dormant during the winter

Biennial
A plant which grows from seed in one season and flowers and dies the following year

Biological controls
Predators which are encouraged to reduce pests, such as nematodes which help to control vine weevil larvae

Bolting
When a plant produces flowers or seeds too soon

Catch crop
A quick growing vegetable (such as radishes) grown at the same time, or between plantings of the main crop

Chitting
To encourage the sprouting of seed potatoes by placing them somewhere light before planting

Cloche
A portable, clear structure designed to protect plants from cold weather

Companion planting
Planting crops close together so that they support one another, such as through pest control or pollination

Crop rotation
Growing different types of crops on the same land each year to reduce disease and balance the demands upon the soil

Dead heading
The removal of dead or faded flowers to encourage the production of more flowers as opposed to seeds

Dibber
Something used to make a small hole in the soil ready to take a seedling

Earthing up
Piling up soil around a plant as it grows

Fertiliser
Something which adds nutrients to soil – maybe a liquid or solid

Germination
The process in which a plant starts to grow from a seed

Grafting
The joining of two plants, usually the rootstock of one with the scion of another

Ground cover
Plants used to create a covering over the soil to suppress weeds

Green manure
A crop grown specifically to add nutrients and improve the structure of the soil

Hardening off
The gradual acclimatisation of a plant to being outside in colder conditions

Hardiness
The ability of a plant to survive in different growing conditions. In the UK plants are generally hardy (ie tolerate frost), half-hardy or tender

Herbaceous
Soft woody plants that lose their leaves over the winter but regrow in the spring

Leaf mould
Compost made from leaves used to improve soil structure or as a mulch

Manure
Animal or plant waste used to feed the soil

Mulch
A layer of natural material spread across the surface of the soil to suppress weeds and conserve water

Organic gardening
An approach which improves the soil and maximises plant health and production without the use of chemical pesticides or artificial fertilisers

Perennial
A plant that lives for several years, dying back in the autumn and winter

Pests
Animals which harm plants

pH
A measure of how acidic or alkaline the soil is

Pinching out
Removing the growing tip to keep a plant compact and more bushy

Pot bound
A plant that has been in a pot too long with compacted roots

Potting on
Moving a plant to a bigger pot as it grows

Potting up
Putting a plant or seed in a pot

Pricking out
Moving seedlings into pots as they grow to give them more space

Propagator
A plastic tray with a clear lid for growing seeds, which may be heated

Root stock
The base and roots of a plant or tree used for grafting another plant onto

Scion
The top part of a tree or plant which is grafted onto the rootstock

Sets
Small onions planted to grow larger onions

Succession sowing
Sowing seeds regularly to ensure a continual crop

Thinning out
The removal of some seedlings to give others more room

Truss
A cluster of fruits at the end of a stem, eg tomatoes

Notes

Notes